An Exclusive Education

Race, Class and Exclusion in
British Schools

An Exclusive Education

Race, Class and Exclusion in British Schools

CHRIS SEARLE

Lawrence & Wishart
LONDON 2001

Lawrence and Wishart Limited
99a Wallis Road
London
E9 5LN

First published 2001

British Library Cataloguing in Publication Data.
A catalogue record for this book is available from the British
Library

ISBN 0 85315 932 7

Text setting Derek Doyle and Associates, Liverpool
Printed and bound by The Bath Press, Bath

CONTENTS

I would like to thank my colleague at Goldsmiths' College, University of London, Paul Dash, for generously contributing his apt and insightful cover design; Patricia Hardwicke for the excellence of her word processing; Gillian Klein for her editing skills and critical encouragement – and Professor Clyde Chitty, editor of *Forum* Journal, for his friendship and the inspiration of his brave tenacity. Also thanks to Sheffield Historian Bill Moore for the example of his life of scholarly struggle – and to Pearl and the boys for their tolerance of, to put it mildly, my eccentricities. Finally, to Sally Davison of Lawrence & Wishart, for her hard work and the pride I feel at being published by an imprint of such telling history.

An Exclusive Education is dedicated to all who have been excluded from school, and have, despite this rejection, struggled to find their own pathways in education and life. Any royalties paid to the author of this book will go to UNICEF (the United Nation's Children's Fund).

Chris Searle, May 2001

INTRODUCTION

The most recent government statistics (for the year 1998-9) reveal that there were 10,404 children permanently excluded from British schools in that year. The aim of this book is to analyse why exclusions are such a menace, to put forward policies to reverse this situation, and to look at wider questions of educational exclusion – for instance exclusion through the curriculum. Educational exclusion is often part of wider processes of political and social exclusion, and this means that any serious attempt to redress this reality must look closely at education. At present, the application of the rules of competition and the market to education, together with the imposition of a National Curriculum which in no way reflects the diversity of children's experiences, means that exclusions are likely to remain a problem in the foreseeable future. This book starts from the premise that each child's life is precious: no child should be treated as expendable - as part of the human waste of the education market, the detritus of league tables and of the frantic inter-school competition for results. An alternative educational strategy is to aim towards an inclusive school, and a system which caters for all our children, and this should be the aim of any democratic society.

National figures show that African-Caribbean boys are at 3-4 times greater risk of permanent exclusion from school than the average – and in some LEAs such as Trafford and Surrey the risk rises fifteen times. In Lancashire towns such as Bolton and Bury, Pakistani boys faced twice the average risk.[1] Primary school children represent one eighth of the overall exclusion figures, a figure which is on the increase.[2] Other troubling research conclusions were reached in a study by the National Foundation for Educational Research, which showed that high exclusion rates were not confined to African Caribbean boys. Other black children were also suffering disproportionately – in particular African Caribbean girls and Bangladeshi boys, as well as children 'statemented' for special educational needs support.[3] In one local educational authority studied, statemented pupils accounted for 20 per cent of excluded youngsters but only 2 per cent of the school population.

Exclusion from school has now become firmly established as a mainstream social and political issue, on both sides of the Atlantic. In the USA at the end of 1999, ex-presidential candidate and civil rights campaigner Jesse Jackson was arrested and handcuffed while picketing outside Eisenhower High School in Decatur, Illinois. He was protesting against the permanent exclusion of six black students and the 'zero tolerance' regime of the local school board, which was bearing down disproportionately on black students. 'It is an honour to be arrested for a righteous cause', he declared as he was taken to jail in a police van, evoking memories of earlier struggles for civil rights. Jackson continued by setting out the structure of a status quo familiar in British cities: 'The schools are 48 per cent black and brown. The teachers and the board are 90 per cent white. This is what happens when you have these culture gaps and stereotypes and unfounded fears'.[4]

Such fears are alive in liberal England. Concern about the

numbers of excluded children is often displaced by fear of crime. In an article in *The Guardian* in April 2000, 'Children from Hell', columnist Polly Toynbee recognised the contours of a serious national issue. 'The figures are frightening,' she wrote, having studied a report from the National Association of the Care and Re-settlement of Offenders (NACRO): 'The Metropolitan Police estimates that 40 per cent of robberies, 25 per cent of all burglaries and 20 per cent of thefts are committed by school-age children during school hours. Truanting or excluded, they roam the streets with nothing to do and nowhere to go: they are the crime wave, not waving but drowning.' After considering the basic pros and cons of school exclusion, the liberal language dissipates into more warlike figures of speech: 'Exclusion has to be an important part of the armoury of any school trying to keep a grip'. NACRO itself concluded, in the words of Paul Cavadino, its policy director, that despite school exclusion frequently being the result of delinquent behaviour, it can also be the cause of it.'[5]

Alongside the serious situation regarding school exclusions there has been a crisis in truancy. In May 2000, a study undertaken among 24 member countries by the Organisation for Economic Co-operation and Development (OECD), showed that England had the sixth worst truancy figures, and Scotland had higher rates of absenteeism from school among 13-year-olds than any other industrialised country.[6] I would argue that exclusion and truancy rates are part of the same problem – the failure to provide an educational structure which is sufficiently motivating and responsive to the needs of all children. Whether officially or unofficially excluded, children who reject education because it appears to be rejecting them can easily become involved in crime and further trouble, both in and out of school. It is important to recognise that this is a problem for the children in trouble as well as for those who are victims of crime.

There have been contradictory responses to the high number of exclusions. The National Association of Headteachers blames the increase on policies of seeking to include more special needs students into mainstream schools, and on 'the mad dash to integrate' such students 'on the cheap'. Their general secretary claims that this is fast creating an 'educational underclass'.[7] In opposition to this, the Children's Society (a voluntary society sponsored by the Church of England) has stated that the high rates of absenteeism from school expose a situation of 'state-sanctioned truancy'.[8]

The Government have responded in a number of ways to this crisis. One (by now habitual) strategy is to resort to the institution of 'league tables' – this time for local education authorities – in order to expose which schools are excluding most students.[9] More recently they have established among local police forces and education authorities special task forces, to execute spot-checks on groups of school-age children found during school time in town centres and city streets, and subsequently to escort truants back to their schools. As the *Star* in Sheffield reported, typifying the approach in many English urban areas: 'A city-wide crackdown on pupils "wagging off" school will be launched by Sheffield's new anti-truancy task force. Groups of youths in their favourite hang-outs will be targeted by teams of police and council truancy officers.'[10] Thus the state school system is once more being associated with authoritarian and military-style operations, and is involved in forcibly 'rounding up' the disaffected, rebellious and alienated youth, the majority of whom are from black and working-class communities. Instead of trying to understand and address the underlying causes of disaffection, there is increasing resort to control and punishment.

NARRATIVES OF EXCLUSION

Inside these figures of school students rejecting and being rejected from the mainstream schooling system of the nation are a host of individual narratives which illustrate the various parts being played by school students, their parents, classroom teachers, headteachers and teacher trade union leaders. There is, for example, the story of Sarah, who was studying for her GCSE examinations at Queen Elizabeth Endowed School in Mansfield, Nottinghamshire, and was one of six students who wrote to a local newspaper criticising what they viewed as poor teaching standards at the school; they claimed that this – in addition to high staff absences – was adversely affecting their education.[11] The headteacher excluded Sarah for her temerity, provoking attention from the national press as well as much local publicity. The head's managerial despotism also directly affected teachers, who, with strong support from the National Union of Teachers, passed a motion of no confidence in her. In the meantime, the criticism of Sarah and her classmates appeared to be vindicated by a very critical OFSTED report (1996) – which highlighted the very points they had made. Sarah was later reinstated in the school.

Then there was the far less sanguine story of fourteen-year-old Niki Crane of Hesketh Bank in Lancashire.[12] Niki is brain-damaged but his parents have been determined to ensure that he receives a mainstream education, and that they will tackle any marginalisation that may intrude upon his life at school – despite the opposition of their local education authority and its insistence that Niki must go to a special school. Considering that nearly one-third of the British people consider that disabled people are less intelligent than the able-bodied, according to an national opinion poll released in May 1997,[13] Mr and Mrs Crane's brave efforts for their son were more than understandable. Mr Crane asserted that 'schools were not comprehensive if they chose pupils on the basis of their ability or disability', and his mother added that 'Niki cannot understand why he cannot go to the comprehensive. He has done nothing wrong'. The parents' campaign was supported by an educational psychologist and a local lecturer in education who were compelled to spend a night in jail after they had occupied Preston education authority offices for two days and lain down in front of local council vehicles. Here, the government shibboleth of 'parental choice' has been selectively discarded – resulting in £50,000 legal costs to Mr and Mrs Crane, who were forced to sell their family home in order to defray them – thus rendering Niki, his sister and his parents homeless as well as school-less. Mr and Mrs Crane had made it clear that at his primary school 'Niki made miraculous progress', learning 'to behave properly by being permanently with other pupils'. Now his sister and friends would be going on to the mainstream school, and he would be barred, leaving his family perplexed, sad and bankrupt.

Home tutor Liz McDonald, recounting the true tale of one of her pupils, in the journal of the National Union of Teachers,[14] points out that 40 per cent of excluded students never re-enter full-time schooling. Her article ends with the assertion that her principled commitment to inclusive education would make her willingly unemployed:

> Harry, my youngest pupil at seven, had been abused by his apparently absent father, and was excluded for 'sexually inappropriate behaviour'. My own son was the same age. It was

painful comparing their environments. Harry's home had no dad, no decent food, no books or intact toys, no music, no pictures on walls, no outings, no holidays, no friends calling in, and worst of all, his mum gave him no time. Conversations were purely functional. Harry could barely string words together, he was not expected to. He must have viewed me as an alien full of incomprehensible sounds. I could not voice anger with his mother: that way led to a closed door next visit.

When Harry was ill, which was often, she would refuse lifts to the doctor's, being wary of professionals 'talking posh'. Since I was the only outsider tolerated, I just kept going, four times weekly, ensuring that he was still alive, and not being abused. On the good days, I taught him to read. It was a relief, after six months, when Harry was placed in a centre for children with 'emotional and behavioural disorders'. They could begin to attend to problems arising in Harry's 'invisible' period, his rotting teeth, damaged hearing, and sores caused by poor nutrition – and they were just the visible signs of his appalling neglect.

There are satisfactions. One can boost shattered self-esteem, and show the pupil that, through mutual respect, he can manage a reasonable relationship with an adult. Harry learned to read, and that was joyously satisfying for both of us. But, on reflection, I would rather be jobless, seeing necessary exclusion followed by prompt re-schooling, than witness the depressing, danger-prone inactivity of a youngster uprooted from his education, friendships and his place in society.

The label 'excluded' weighs him down like an albatross.

The humanity and empathy of this teacher trade union member – her professional concern, compassion and hugely loving approach to excluded students – is in stark contrast with the position of Nigel de Gruchy, General Secretary of the National Association of Schoolmasters and Union of Women Teachers (NASUWT), as illustrated in the following case. Matthew Wilson, a troubled 10-year-old from Manton Junior School in Worksop, Nottinghamshire, was, according to the *Daily Mail*, 'the boy they can't tame'.[15] The *Sun* called him a 'yob'[16] and the *Daily Express* 'a little horror'.[17] The usually more temperate *Guardian* reported that he was 'uncontrollable'.[18] In fact, Matthew was trying to deal with the recent death of his father, his mother's onset of cancer and the death of two other close family members. Excluded, then reinstated by a properly constituted appeals committee, a majority of his teachers refused to teach him, strongly supported by the NASUWT. The chair of Matthew's school governors stood firmly on the boy's side; 'He is a challenge', she said, 'but a bright and nice boy'. Parent governors and others associated with the school also refused to abandon him after his bereavements, although they knew he was frequently a difficult and challenging pupil. 'He is no pushover – he answers back', declared one. 'But if you reason with him he is perfectly all right'. A school meals assistant added that 'he can be a little monkey and a bit of a handful, but he is not on his own at the school at being like that'.[19] They wanted to continue to educate him at the school, and help him improve and progress in his relationships.

Contrarily, the NASUWT threatened to release confidential documents about the boy and led its teachers in a strike and boycott against him. De Gruchy declared:

> If they keep on saying in public he is a sweet little devil we might have to release the whole dossier. We don't want to do that because it makes his life more difficult, but we might have to. So long as our members are protected and don't have

anything to do with him, teaching, in corridors or at playtime, that will be acceptable. If those conditions are not met, and unless they can come up with an alternative and his parent does the sensible thing and withdraws him from school, we will be back to strike action.[20]

As a tailpiece to Matthew's saga, after his 'battle-weary' mother had moved him to another school, his new teachers found him to be most receptive and co-operative – describing him as 'well-adjusted, highly motivated, polite and helpful'.[21] They found it difficult to understand what all the fuss had been about. Thus, his demonisation appeared not only a local teachers' ploy to justify exclusion, but also a nationwide fabrication, which he and his family will be left to contemplate as he grows older.

The experiences of Sandra Robbins, a cleaner, and her nine-year old son John, related in *The Times Educational Supplement*,[22] are both harrowing and instructive, and show the visceral effect that exclusion has on a family, as well as an individual child. John, a middle child, had no education at all for his first three months of exclusion, until his local education authority organised two home tuition sessions a week – described by his mother as comprising 'a few sums and some dot-to-dot pictures'. Even at the stage of his exclusion he was a full two academic years behind his classmates and found it very difficult to make friendships with them. As for Sandra, she was forced by circumstances to give up her job and live on income support. She stayed at home looking after her son, who, unable to go to school, became 'bored witless'. John would follow his mother around their council home, kicking his heels and becoming more and more frustrated. 'By the weekend, I'm absolutely finished,' Sarah declared, 'it's doing my head in'. Much of her week is frequently spent on the telephone to local education officers, trying to regain her rights and a full-time education for her son. 'You ring up and they aren't in, and they put you on to someone else, and they tell you that the person that you have to speak to isn't in the office and someone'll let you know. And then you wait and wait and wait and nothing happens'. She is told the switchboard is down, the files are unobtainable, the offices are being re-organised or the relevant officer is sick or at a meeting. A nightmare of local state bureaucracy prevents her from achieving the one prize which should be her inalienable right: a full-time state education for her child.

The reality of 'exclusion' now exerts a profound influence over British state education. Physical exclusion from school is a tangible reality which negatively affects many working-class and black families, impacting greatly on their children's progress in (or out of) school. As was documented by the former South London school students who wrote their life-narratives in *This is Where I Live*, many a drift into youthful criminal activity has been 'engendered by exclusion from school'.[23] In this sense 'exclusion' used as a sanction is frequently an early route to the frustrating and spoiling of life's chances for urban young people.

EXCLUSION AS SYMPTOM

One of the central arguments of *This Where I Live* is that the physical exclusion of students from school, with all its attendant damage to the life chances of each child, needs to be seen in the context of a wider culture of exclusion. Exclusion also involves what is and *isn't* there in our schools: what schools offer, or to use the more official and jargonised word 'deliver', within their curriculum particular systems of institutional morality and overall ethos. This often means that children feel excluded, in a deeper sense, even while they remain in school. They are excluded by what they are commanded to learn and by much of the prescribed body of knowledge, which often relates to them only inasmuch as it humiliates and ignores them. They are frequently excluded by prevailing attitudes towards race, class, gender, language, history, religion, culture and the essential features of the communities to which they belong. They are expected, in the action of assimilating approved and state-licensed knowledge, to swallow and believe caricatures of themselves, racist interpretations of who they are, what they believe, the words they speak, the struggles that their people have waged and the achievements that they have generated in this and former societies elsewhere in the world where their origins may lie, and members of their families continue to live. They are instructed on 'how to live', by a false morality which gives greater significance to individual advancement and competitive social relations than it does to ways of making union, creating community esteem and securing safe and generous futures for those who live now, and those who will make their own rendezvous with the future. There is one large northern 'specialist' secondary school, for example, where the headteacher's favourite slogan, 'The more you learn, the more you earn', is the regular theme of school assemblies.

Physical exclusion from school is signally the reward for resistance at school. Often that resistance is anarchic, even barbarous, and teachers inevitably find themselves on the receiving end. It can be very difficult to cope with, but what needs to be understood is that such resistance is the hostile reaction to feeling not only excluded, but insulted, denied human respect, ignored or rendered invisible as a cultured human being. It is a reaction to a realisation that, although you know your language, history, religion or culture are all huge, sustaining – and worthy of learning – none of them matter to an established school culture that speaks of things and values British and European and endorses little else. Your anger provokes you to question and resist, and this brings the familiar disciplinary consequences. As one Brixton youth argues, 'As black kids, we tend to ask why. I used to argue certain things, not because I wanted to cause trouble, but because I wanted to get it straight in my head'.[24] Another adds, 'when teachers gave instructions or orders without any explanation or discussion, the alienated youths responded to it in ways which were negatively interpreted. From there the trouble escalated'.

Young people are frequently shattered personally, and institutionally, when a school – which beyond all things purports to offer knowledge, insight and lucidity – appears to teach them the opposite, in relation to those human truths based in their families and communities that give them confidence, pride and succour as human beings. They are told that their language doesn't matter or is inferior; their history is dismissed or hidden from them; their writers and singers go unmentioned, unstudied or unlisted on curriculum programmes; their religion is rejected or caricatured as fanatical; and their family life or cultural origins are relegated to the uncivilised. Yet much of this, and more, is to be found within the narrow tramlines of the 'National Curriculum', with what is precious in their lives and histories frequently excised and excluded. It creates pain and an intense alienation from school and school-prescribed knowledge. In such a context, it is not surprising that a large proportion of black young people at state schools – forty per cent, to be precise, from the evidence of one survey[25] – stated that were one to be available, they would much prefer to be studying at an all-black school, where there would at least be the opportunity of an ethos and curriculum that would affirm their human life and culture, and give them the self-esteem and confidence that should be the edifice upon which all education is developed. Twenty per cent also thought that they had recently suffered racism directly from a teacher.[26]

That exclusion connects fundamentally with issues of race and racism across British schools is clearly evident; but it also continuously intersects with basic issues of class. The dominant culture within schools, as in society more widely, is that of the middle- and upper-class establishment. It is taken for granted that what should be celebrated and handed on are the achievements of the dominant groups within society. The curriculum implications of this will be explored in a later chapter. But they are well illustrated in a 1998 dispute over naming a new city centre public garden in the Yorkshire ex-industrial city of Sheffield. This dispute highlights the ways in which memorialising the rich and prosperous is seen as natural. To challenge such memorialism, and to assert the right of the working class or other marginalised groups to be remembered and celebrated, is an important part of a struggle for the recognition and inclusion of subordinated cultures – whether these cultures are defined by class, race or any other inequality.

In 1998, Sheffield's Labour city council proposed to name its new gardens after the prosperous local industrialist and philanthropist Sir Stuart Goodwin. This decision provoked resistance amongst those whose sense and study of history told them that Sheffield was essentially a working-class city, built on the labour of ordinary people working in the mills and workshops of the huge steel and cutlery industries established in the city through the nineteenth and early twentieth centuries. The argument was that this was the history of the majority, and this was what should be remembered. One of the main campaigners was retired teacher and labour historian Bill Moore, now in his ninetieth year. Moore helped to set up the Holberry Society in 1978, to celebrate the contribution to Sheffield of Samuel Holberry, a Chartist who led a failed revolt in the city in 1840. After Holberry died of consumption in York Prison in 1842, Sheffield stopped work, the shops closed and 50,000 Sheffielders lined the streets for the funeral procession – echoing the truth that Chartism was a popular mass movement that had secured over a million signatures for its petition in support of the Charter that was handed to the government of the day. Moore argued that Holberry was one of many people who had made a much greater contribution to the history of Sheffield than Sir Stuart Goodwin. He argued that the choice a government, local or national, makes with regard to the narratives and figures it chooses to characterise its history is a fundamental one. Who is vindicated, who is excluded? People such as Holberry are not only not celebrated in our public squares; their contribution is ignored in school curricula and hence in our sense of who we are and what matters to us.[27]

This is an extract from one of Moore's representations

It irritates me that this honour is being given to a man whose only contribution to the city was to make a fortune out of it and then give some of the money back. The new gardens should commemorate the history of Sheffield people over the past hundred years, the way they have organised the struggle – not just the struggle for democratic rights, but general human rights. A philanthropist just can't hold a candle to it. Holberry is a symbol of the people – the *real* Sheffield, the *real* source of Sheffield's renown. My grandmother remembered people talking about Holberry twenty years after he died. But the thing that depresses me is lack of knowledge. Every child in Sheffield should know they come from a fighting city. But no-one teaches them the wonderful history of the Sheffield working class. This city had the first trades council in the world, fighting for the end of slavery forty years before it was ended in the British Empire. These were the people who made Sheffield a by-word for excellence throughout the world.[28]

Moore's lament for the lack of knowledge in state schools about the activities of millions of people who supported social progress, the right to vote and share power with each other – and the inspiration and self-sacrifice of their leaders – relates to a fundamental dimension of exclusion in British schools. The resources of state education, as of public culture more widely, exclude vast areas of knowledge and curriculum.

This is reflected in the narrow and restrictive National Curriculum which, in defining what is worthy of inclusion, manages to exclude immense stores of knowledge considered as being of lesser status, or irrelevant to the mainsprings of a national culture, or dangerous, subversive or critical. The imposition of the National Curriculum, through its formalisation of a traditional view of what is of cultural and hence educational value, is dispossessing millions of young people of a cognitive foundation which belongs to them and their communities. The National Curriculum is immensely prescriptive, and closes down some of the opportunities that previously existed for local communities and schools to challenge dominant conceptions of what should be taught. It has all the apparatus of the state behind it – the Department of Education and the Environment (DfEE), OFSTED and other powerful and associated educational quangos together form the superstructures and infrastructures of state education machinery and surveillance. With such state machinery a nation 'fixes' its knowledge, decides what is to be included and what is to be excluded, and prescribes and licenses its curricula across its system of schools. In large, predominantly working-class cities like Sheffield, the majority of its people are excised from being the makers and protagonists of their own lives and histories: hence class becomes the main agency of exclusion. They can learn about the other, but not about themselves: the rich philanthropist is celebrated while the working-class rebel is subordinated and marginalised. People from other marginalised groups are even more neglected – for example Mary Holberry, who was also a crucial participant in the Sheffield Chartist movement, and an outstanding organiser and creator of history in her own right, or William Cuffay, who was an influential black Chartist.

The thousands of children formally excluded from school on a permanent basis do not signal the boundaries of exclusion but its starting point; they are the emblems not the limits. The system that has rejected them also rejects thousands of others, in different ways, and rejects the knowledge and ethos which could motivate and fulfil them as learning human beings.

'BEHAVIOURAL CLEANSING'

Although neither Labour nor the Conservatives recognise that exclusion is actively promoted by educational policies based on competitiveness and a narrow view of the curriculum, they have different strategies for dealing with the crisis. These strategies are as much influenced by populist considerations as educational concerns.

In 2000, for New Labour the priority was to meet its stated target on the 'reduction' of exclusions, and it promised to bring down the existing total of 12,300 permanent exclusions nationally by one third by the year 2002. Part of its strategy to achieve this was announced by David Blunkett at the April conference of the pro-exclusion NASUWT. '1000 sin bins to curb the unruly', headlined *The Times Educational Supplement*[29] in its report of Blunkett's 'crackdown on tearaways'. In language clearly constructed to appeal to NASUWT delegates, Blunkett told the assembly: 'Whether it is bullying, threatening or violent behaviour, abusive and insulting language or an impression of anarchy and lawlessness, we must act.' Forty-seven million pounds was to be dedicated for the establishing of 'learning support units' attached to schools, which would add 580 more to the already existing 420 units. Sixty of the new centres were to be for primary school children.

This was Blunkett setting out resources for an approach of 'internal exclusion'. The students assigned to the units were to be confined in them within their schools and offered an individualised 'educational behaviour plan', and were to be excluded from their normal classes with their peers until such time as their behaviour was judged to be more acceptable for mainstream lessons. That such units were known and openly described nationally – even by the respectable educational press – as 'sin bins' clearly indicated their stigma; and this would be applied, of course, to all who studied within them or turned up to their activities. But this degree of exclusion was still not sufficient for the NASUWT. General Secretary Nigel de Gruchy's response to Blunkett's plans was to tell him to 'Get real!'.[30] He declared that his members wanted 'zero tolerance of bad behaviour', and advocated the creation of many more 'pupil referral units', which should be detached and self-contained, with their pupils kept sufficiently far away not to pollute mainstream schools. As *The Guardian* reported,[31] de Gruchy did not want 'to leave the disruptive children free to hang around the gates' of normal

schools. They were to be behaviourally cleansed, their influence to be transported well away from the majority of their
former schoolmates. They were to become the new pariahs.
For Paul Macey, writing his perspective on the Blunkett
internal exclusion strategy in the black weekly, *The Voice*,[32] it
amounted to a virtual ethnic cleansing, since black students
were so blatantly and disproportionately excluded across the
schools of England. He quoted Sandra Johnson of the Leeds-
based Community Action for Education:

> These proposals will reinforce our children's low esteem. The
> language implies that children in these units will be rubbish.
> The money made available in these proposals should be given
> to black projects, which will care for and support the children
> to achieve their aspirations.

Hard on the heels of the New Labour exclusion plans
came Leader of the Opposition William Hague's
Conservative Party alternative. This was given a strong
endorsement on the BBC's *Question Time* by the then Chief
Inspector of OFSTED, Chris Woodhead. 'Hague's rival sin-
bin plan for violent pupils' – as *The Times* announced it
through a front-page headline [33] – advocated the retreat to a
nationwide network of out-of-school 'progress centres' for
excluded students, approximating very closely to the
NASUWT blueprint for physical exclusion, even quarantine.
In the media imagination, too, the notion of an 'excluded'
student began to fuse with a 'violent' student, so successful
had been the NASUWT caricature. Hague was quite determined that these excluded 'young thugs' would not 'hold our
classrooms to ransom' – a cliché more usually applied to
striking teachers. He promised that, once elected, he would
abolish New Labour's targets for cutting exclusion in main-

stream schools and 'give headteachers and governors complete freedom, within the law, to set their own standards and discipline rules' (powers which they already have anyway). He also offered a policy which had become something of an obsession with de Gruchy and the NASUWT – the final abolition of LEA appeals panels, which are the only remedy parents can use to contest the exclusion, unfair or otherwise, of their sons or daughters.

In July 2000 a High Court judge decided to set aside an appeals panel decision which had allowed an excluded fourteen-year-old boy to continue to attend his Essex school. His headteacher had permanently excluded him for allegedly hitting a fellow student in a dinner queue.[34] A day after this decision, the New Labour schools' minister Jacqui Smith stated that appeals panels should not reinstate excluded students if they had transgressed 'an explicit discipline policy' of their school. She named a gamut of offences where the decisions of appeals panels should have no effect, some clearly much more serious than others, including 'serious violence, drug dealing, sex abuse and repeated flouting of uniform rules.'[35] Thus was the only avenue of redress for parents of excluded students all but closed through a combination of High Court and government dictat. Education correspondents in many newspapers reported de Gruchy's glee: he took the opportunity to declare that 'they should go the whole hog and abolish these appeals panels completely.'[36] The National Association of Headteachers' General Secretary observed that the new ruling made the Government's lower exclusions target 'a dead duck';[37] an editorial in the *Guardian* warmly greeted this 'greater leeway' for heads; and the *Times*, the *Mail* and the *Independent* all welcomed this 'exclusions U-turn' and agreed that it left the Government's exclusions strategy 'in tatters'.[38] Not without a sense of triumphalism, *The Times* leader opined that 'the rights of a child must no longer be placed ahead of the good of a school'.[39]

EXCLUSION AND POPULISM

That exclusion from school has become such a crucial part of a populist educational agenda only illustrates how far state education has become detached from rational and critical debate. Nowhere amongst the spin and rhetoric of either party, or from within the unrighteous indignation of the NASUWT, has there been any real attempt to look inwards at school organisation, curriculum and pedagogy, or to develop strategies to motivate the marginalised urban youth most vulnerable to exclusion, to draw them into educational dialogue or schemes for genuine learning development. The response to the exclusion issue has degenerated into crude caricatures of those who are excluded and accusations against them and their parents and communities. It is also frequently contemptuous of the dedicated and creative work engaged in by thousands of teachers in the most unpromising of educational environments. It has become almost anathema to criticise the new orthodoxies. The National Curriculum is now a shibboleth for both parties, and its over-prescribed content of cultural, linguistic and nationalist exclusiveness is rarely considered. The return of transmissive, didactic and anti-dialogic pedagogies is now due to rise up through the school system, following their consolidation in the 'Literacy Hours' and 'Numeracy Hours' in primary schools: the same narrow approaches are being institutionalised in secondary schools too. The convergent behaviourism underpinning many 'school improvement' and 'school effectiveness' programmes is becoming the antidote to creativity and spontaneity in learning, and much else that is valuable in school life, as 'control' and 'conformity' become the new agenda. The constant threat of an impending OFSTED inspection is becoming a severe menace to adventure, audacity and experiment in teaching – and the kind of pedagogical risks teachers need to take to stimulate and provoke the imagination and motivation of their most unwilling students. At the time of writing, the Government's plans to reintroduce selective education through the setting up of 'specialist' schools look set to drive one more nail into the coffin of comprehensive education. Their use of the term 'bog standard' to describe comprehensive schools is symptomatic both of their contempt for ordinary teachers and children and their more general educational elitism. The contradictions of the authoritarian view of education which centrally prescribes what should be taught and the 'enterprise' approach which loudly proclaims choice have perhaps never been more poignant. Such policies are the logical outcome of an educational approach which seeks to out-Tory the Tories. As Blunkett admitted – with some recourse to euphemism – on BBC *Newsnight* (12.2.01): 'The Tories had one or two ideas which we've built on'.

Most teachers recognise that the need for a critical pedagogy has never been more pressing, but also that it has never been more discouraged: the full participation of teachers and learners in the construction of classroom curriculum has never been more urgent – but, because of the National Curriculum, never more forbidden. From becoming true meeting places of curriculum and community, with each feeding and sustaining the other, classrooms are becoming 'delivery' rooms for state-licensed knowledge; as such they are policed and contained by OFSTED (which, incidentally has been strongly criticised by the Commission for Racial Equality for ignoring racism in its school inspections[40]), and by many colluding school management and governing bodies, preoccupied as they are by examination results and elevated positions on local league tables, often at the expense of their most needy and demotivated students. A new research report published by the Children's Society warned that school students are being compelled to sit as many as 75 examinations between the ages of four and eighteen, provoking many more cases of examophobia, resulting in panic attacks, acute sleeplessness and eating disorders.[41]

This book seeks to tackle the issue of school exclusion by identifying a number of its primary dimensions. Starting off from physical exclusion from school as a sanction (and never straying far from this most visceral manifestation), it moves on to reflect upon exclusion in curriculum terms and in aspects of the new 'moralism', as well as the structures and conventions which schools systemically use to exclude internally. In doing this, the author frequently uses his own educational life and experiences as pupil, teacher and head-teacher as a kind of case profile. Finally, there is a chapter on what a truly comprehensive and inclusive school might involve and genuinely include. For that is this teacher's real objective in teaching and learning: an end to 'outcast England' in education, as in all other dimensions of its social and institutional life.

REFERENCES

1. *Times Educational Supplement*, 11.12.98.
2. Carol Hayden, *Children Excluded from Primary School: Debates, Evidence, Response*, Open University Press, 1998.
3. *Times Educational Supplement*, 18.2.00.
4. *Guardian*, 18.11.99.
5. *Morning Star,* 13.4.00.
6. *Daily Mail*, 17.5.00.

7. *Guardian*, 31.10.97.

8. *Guardian*, 31.10.97.

9. *Education Guardian*, 12.5.98.

10. *Star*, Sheffield, 15.6.00.

11. *The Teacher*, December 1997.

12. *Guardian*, 13.5.97.

13. *The Times*, 26.5.98.

15. *Daily Mail*, 28.8.96.

16. *Sun*, 28.8.96.

17. *Daily Express*, 28.8.96.

18. *Guardian*, 31.10.96.

19. *Daily Mail*, 31.10.96.

20. *Guardian*, 4.9.96.

21. *Guardian*, 30.8.97.

22. *Times Educational Supplement*, 24.4.98.

23. *This is Where I Live: Stories and Pressures in Brixton,* London, The Runnymede Trust, 1996.

24. *Ibid.*

25. *Guardian*, 27.10.97.

26. Some instructive case studies of exclusion and the culture in which they have developed are set down in the excellent publication of the 'Race on the Agenda' group, *Inclusive Schools, Inclusive Society*, written and compiled by Robin Richardson and Angela Wood (Trentham Books, Stoke-on-Trent, 1999). Other case studies are described in *Outcast England: How Schools Exclude Black Children*, edited by Jenny Bourne, Lee Bridges and Chris Searle (Institute of Race Relations, London 1994).

27. The determination and tenacity of Bill Moore and his Holberry Society Colleagues bore fruit when the Sheffield City Council decided that the tributary fountains leading to the main Goodwin Fountain should be named the 'Holberry Cascades'. Moore was invited to dedicate the memorial plaque, which he

hoped would become 'a reminder of all those so often forgotten Sheffield men and women who carried on the struggle and never gave in'.

28. *Sheffield Telegraph*, 24.4.98.
29. *Times Educational Supplement*, 28.4.00.
30. *Guardian*, 27.4.00.
31. *Guardian*, as above.
32. *Voice*, 8.5.00.
33. *Times*, 6.6.00.
34. *Guardian*, 1.8.00.
35. *Independent*, 2.8.00.
36. *Daily Mail*, 2.8.00.
37. *Daily Mail*, 2.8.00.
38. *Independent*, 2.8.00.
39. *Times*, 2.8.00.
40. *Evening Standard*, 17.7.00, reporting on the response to research done by Leicester University based on a study of more than 10,000 OFSTED inspection reports.
41. *Morning Star*, 4.8.00.

CHAPTER 1

Exclusion and Division in the Postwar School System

There is a convincing argument that the entire modern school system of Britain has been built upon exclusion. Its processes informed the structure of education set in motion by the 1944 Education Act, with its the separation of secondary schools according to dubious categories of 'ability', a system which still continues in those parts of Britain which have retained the primacy of the 'eleven-plus' examination. Later, comprehensive schools seemed to promise to get rid of this divisiveness, but new systems and processes have continued to ensure that exclusion, rejection and built-in failure are the educational experience of thousands of young British people. The promotion of internal setting, streaming and 'fast-track' routes, to reassure middle-class parents anxious about comprehensive schools, has meant that the old structural educational divisions are now frequently to be found under one school roof. Current government insistence is upon maintaining 'diversity' among schools – with the proposed introduction of further 'specialist' schools to add to an already existing repertoire of neighbourhood comprehensives, 'technology colleges', grant maintained schools and grammar schools.

EDUCATION IN BRITAIN SINCE 1965

The eleven-plus system was challenged in the 1960s and 1970s, through the decisive 1965 circular 10/65 which made the comprehensive reorganisation of secondary schools national policy, so that over time comprehensive education became the experience of most children. It should be noted however that even at the high point of comprehensive education, as Caroline Benn and Clyde Chitty point out in their luminous history of the first thirty years of comprehensive education in Britain, *Thirty Years On*, there was a 'continuum' of division, so that alongside genuinely comprehensive schools there were those that were comprehensive in name only.[1] As well as the spread of comprehensive education, the 1960s and 1970s saw other measures which promoted inclusiveness within schools – such as more inclusive curricula and new and more student-centred methods of teaching. These developments were always contested, however, and from 1979 onwards there began a backlash not only against comprehensive education, but also against the more inclusive policies which were developing in some LEAs. After the 1988 Education Act, which introduced grant maintained schools, the numbers of comprehensive schools in England decreased.

The 1988 Act was a major assault on the gains of the 1960s and 1970s. It inaugurated the dual strategy which is still in place today. On the one hand it introduced a number of measures which, under the guise of parental choice, increased competitive and market pressures within the school system (this reflected the neo-liberal side of the Right's approach); on the other hand, in introducing the National Curriculum, it heavily centralised control, in an attempt to reassert traditional English values which it saw as under threat (and here we see the authoritarian side of their approach). These in many ways contradictory impulses have led to a situation in which education has been continuously subjected to processes of both centralisation (of content) and de-centralisation (of organisation). It should be noted however that successive Secretaries of State have retained wide powers of intervention – it is mainly LEAs which have lost powers. Control of schools has been taken away from LEAs and teachers in a pincer movement that has seen power devolved upwards to government and downwards to governing bodies. Broadly speaking, curriculum control belongs to government, and day-to-day organisation to school governing bodies – although much of the devolution to governing bodies is rhetorical: the framework within which they operate is heavily policed. The centralisation of the curriculum and the institution of market processes each exert pressures which tend to make schools less inclusive.

The 1988 Act brought in a range of measures which put pressure on schools to deter them from pursuing inclusive approaches to education. Local education authorities were no longer able to give substantial 'positive action' funding to hard-pressed inner-city schools; the system of 'catchment areas' for comprehensive schools was brought to an end, and the change to 'open enrolment' created a dash for admission to the well-endowed suburban schools; 'league tables' were instituted to compare and contrast schools' examination success. Schools now had to compete against each other for children to teach, and to sharpen up their public image – sometimes at the expense of educational substance – and they had to become constantly wary, and alert to the interventionist surveillance of OFSTED, whose inspections and follow-up monitoring became increasingly obedient to the Conservative agenda. As schools acted to fit themselves into these new government 'orders', the compulsory new National Curriculum began to prohibit any curriculum expansiveness and cognitive imagination that may have developed. The same formulaic curriculum was imposed upon all schools, irrespective of the differences or diversity in their student populations. Opportunities for teachers to create their own modules for GCSE syllabi and mark them through continuous assessment were also all but removed, so the 'bespoke' approach to curriculum – customising knowledge in direct relation to relevance, student motivation or local emphasis – was also excised. Students had to learn what they were told, as teachers had to teach what they were told. Prescription replaced teacher creativity, and with the theme word becoming 'delivery', the idea of the teacher being a maker and researcher of knowledge in the classroom in collaboration with the students was set aside.

The precise impact of this governmental process and its negative influence on both teachers and students had profound extra-curricular dimensions. As their 'name' and 'image' became all important to schools competing for parental favour and full rolls, more and more of them began to exclude students whom they saw as disrupting the smooth operation of lessons or causing problems for increasingly overworked teachers who were suffering from vastly heavier preparation, documentation and assessment burdens that resulted from the National Curriculum and its regulation by OFSTED. And fewer schools were prepared to take students excluded from other local schools. Teachers found less time to support and counsel students experiencing social, family or personal problems, and schools were less inclined to spend their precious and often diminishing financial resources on pastoral posts, counsellors or community liaison projects. The overall priority now was 'delivering' the National Curriculum and 'securing' successful examination results. The pastoral revolution was over in schools. Troublemakers were expendable and soon began to be 'permanently excluded', dropped like unwanted ballast. The lives and experiences of a large number of students were once more excluded from the curriculum and ethos to be 'delivered' in schools.

'New Labour' in government has done little to change the tendency towards exclusion in education. It has uncritically accepted much previous policy. In particular it delights in the market system in all spheres of society and, if anything, is increasing competitiveness and selectivity within schools. It also shares with the Conservatives an authoritarian impulse towards controlling the curriculum.

The 1944 Education Act set up a system which was divided by the secondary modern and grammar school differential; the wounds of this system were experienced by millions through the 1940s, 1950s and 1960s. In spite of attempts at reform in the 1960s and 1970s we now, at the beginning of the new millennium, have manifold divisions that are structured into our school system in a more sophisticated way. Seven per cent of British young people are still privately educated in privileged fee-paying schools: 163 grammar schools still exist, also 15 'City Technology Colleges', 330 'specialist' schools and 1115 direct grant schools with their higher levels of resourcing.[2] The New Labour government have begun the development of 25 'Education Action Zones', primarily in inner city areas. These are partly financed and governed by such private companies as Kelloggs in Manchester, Shell International in Lambeth (fresh from their spoliation in Nigeria), McDonald's hamburger chain in North Somerset and the National Westminster Bank in the East London Borough of Newham.[3] In Sheffield, the new semi-privatised school opened on the same site as the now closed-down Earl Marshal Comprehensive is to be the flagship of the north-east Sheffield Education Action Zone. Thus, division takes a more subtle expression, and exclusion becomes even more gradated and insidious.

The next two sections of this chapter are based mainly on my own experiences when I was at school, and on those of my students when I later became a teacher. The aim is to look at personal experiences of division and exclusion, and attempts to overcome them. Unfortunately, many of these experiences are not merely of historical interest but are echoed in today's system, which is still divisive in so many ways.

SECONDARY MODERNS AND GRAMMARS

In 1972, when I was a secondary school teacher in East London, I compiled a national anthology of school students' poetry, called *Fire Words*.[4] Of poems that were sent to me from all over Britain, many expressed young people's frustration with schools and the injustice of the school system, which for many at that time still involved selection at eleven-plus. A school-leaver from Manchester supplied a poem which passionately expressed the feelings of one of the majority who failed the eleven plus and was sent to a lower-tier secondary modern school – the 'catch all' of those who were excluded from the 'grammar school' strata. This was the first verse:

> I am one of those Secondary Moderners,
> The ones that the future holds nothing in
> store for.
> Don't anyone tell me I have a future,
> Because I am one of a million fleas
> Trapped in a land of giant bees.
> When I left school my heart was set on
> writing,

When I left school I didn't know that all
   my life I'd be fighting
Something called a working man's ditch,
Where the poor get poorer and the rich get
   richer.
Already my bones begin to ache,
And my mind is drugged to hell with all the
   trash of life, my life.
Already at seventeen my soul begins to
   stretch and awake
And I wish with all my brain
I could go back to sleep again.

Peter Gresty

The glimpse of a likely future is here, mediated through schooling, grounded in class – and interpreted through a pessimistic haze of failure and exclusion. Such a vision was not unusual for many who were sent to secondary modern schools and contrasted with the overweening confidence of the assumptions of those who found themselves on a route to grammar school – such as this eleven-year-old boy from Mexborough in south Yorkshire.

I am going to the Grammar School
Oh! My first day.
You get a lot of homework there
To last you the whole day.
Playing football
This will be fun.
They say there's a gymnasium there
But I don't care.
I've come to work
To get O-levels,

Working all the time,
We'll start half an hour before nine ...
                                    Wayne Graham

My own experience during the 1950s and early 1960s was close to both these writers. Like millions, I failed the eleven-plus – I failed an interview for a grammar school and a re-sit too, as I was considered a 'borderline' failure. My own examination problem was with the 'intelligence tests' in the eleven-plus examinations, designed to establish whether the 'intelligence quotient' (IQ) of the candidate was sufficient to enable him or her to succeed in a grammar school. Like many others, I found great difficulty with these tests. They had become institutionalised in the eleven-plus, following the psychometrical 'revolution' engineered by the research of Cyril Burt and his colleagues during the thirties and forties – later found to be bogus – which implied an 'innate genetic endowment' of intelligence contained within the brain of each child, whose conditioning and life experiences were deemed irrelevant to the working of intelligence. Later, with the research of psychometrists like Arthur Jensen and H. J. Eysenck, these falsely based ideas were to take on profoundly racist dimensions, claiming to establish that black children had lower levels of innate intelligence than their white peers. They were to re-emerge strongly in the nineties through the 'findings' of American social scientists Richard Herrnstein and Charles Murray (1996), and the related arguments of contemporary British academics like the government-favoured James Tooley, who seek to re-impose a universal IQ test for all children at the age of ten. But like millions of my contemporaries and their parents, I had no idea at the time of my eleven-plus experiences of the dubious nature of these tests. I just knew I could not do them, like many of my friends. And yet they became the deciding factor, governing entrance into, or rejection by, the grammar school.

I went to a local secondary modern, spent two years there and, like the rest of my classmates, was offered one last hope of a grammar school transfer at the age of thirteen, through the 'late developers' examination. Following this examination, I was offered an interview for my local grammar school, passed it mainly on the basis of being able to spell correctly the word 'excerpt' to my prospective headteacher, and found myself at the beginning of the next academic year in the newly established 'Remove' stream of the second year of the grammar school, having been put a year behind those of my year group who had made the direct entry from primary school at the age of eleven. There were thirty of us – new, disorientated, a year out of time and sync – and already, it seemed, being steered away, 'removed', from a university future as we were never allowed to study Latin (which at the time was needed to enter most English universities for anybody who aspired to take a degree in an Arts subject).

In the secondary modern there were outside toilets. The 'school library' consisted of four shelves in one cupboard in a classroom, which I exhausted well before the end of the two years I spent there. The school hall served for PE too and had virtually no gymnastics equipment, and for sports we were squeezed into a corner of the nearby girls' grammar school playing fields, which we entered along a narrow path through a builders' yard on a road leading up to the school. We were firmly warned off talking to the girls along the frontier of the playing field, and not allowed to use their entrance. The majority of the students were from working-class families, with the odd boy like myself from a lower-middle-class home, apparently being educated 'below myself'. Yet I remember the teachers with immense admiration and respect. They were dedicated and hard-working – humorous and anecdotal in their classroom style – and because many of them had been emergency trained after active service during the war, their lessons were full of wartime experiences. The geography teacher, for example, served on submarines and laced his lessons with tales of the ocean depths. But because of the same background they also brought a tough, mercilessly authoritarian approach to classroom management, and their attitudes radiated a sense of imperial pride and fixation. I can remember the sense of indignation among the teachers that greeted the news in 1956 of Nasser's seizure of the Suez Canal, and the 'half-hearted' English response by the Eden government. 'We should have gone right in!' I heard some teachers protest. But I learned much there from a skilful and hugely enthusiastic young English teacher recently qualified from a Bristol training college, and a martinet of a music teacher who, against all the odds and meagre resourcing, managed to run a successful school orchestra. I also appreciated the drama tradition in the school, and the opportunities to act in serious productions of adaptations of *Aesop's Fables* and a play about the life of Columbus – in which the name part was played by a hero of the school, the first student (who lived in a local children's home) ever to gain five O-levels.

Years later, after transferring to grammar school and eventually gaining a university degree, I returned to 'apprentice teach' at my old secondary modern, and was hailed by its teachers as a 'success' of the system, something I could only believe with some irony and doubtfulness – for had I stayed there, there was no reason why I would not have gone the way of the millions of others among my contemporaries who spent their years of state education in a secondary modern school – excluded from the main route to examination success and university entry.

When I arrived at the grammar school, I could hardly believe my good fortune, and spent weeks lamenting what my good friends in the school I had left behind were missing. Not only girls too, but a library which was the size of two whole classrooms and covered in shelves. The difference in resources was almost overwhelming. When the library teacher introduced us to the Dewey classification system during our first library lesson, I can recall being bewildered, remembering those four shelves of heavily-fingered books in my previous school. I savoured the superb gymnasium and the three grass cricket pitches (we had had one made of a spongy asphalt in the secondary modern), and could only marvel as teachers wandered the corridors with black gowns and we were given our first-ever lessons in French. I was even given a small part in what seemed a grand production of Sheridan's *The Rivals* during my first year at the school, which would lead to bigger parts in Thornton Wilder's *Our Town* and Brecht's *The Caucasian Chalk Circle*.

Looking back, as I moved out of the orbit of working-class circumscription of my secondary modern school, I could feel myself embracing a different, middle-class destiny in an ethos more attuned to my social reality, fulfilled with O-level and A-level success and the final school year prize of a place at university. Yet when I thought about it, particularly in later years when I became a teacher, I compared my own good fortune with my friends who had carried on in the secondary modern, left at fifteen – or perhaps sixteen, with just a couple of O-levels and then had to make the best of it in the sudden world of work or unemployment.

As to the curriculum of the grammar school, I accepted it unquestioningly alongside almost all of my classmates. Its nationalist assumptions of white superiority and male dominance barely registered. Ours was an all-white suburban school, with little to provoke resistance or challenge, and a preparedness to conform for success. We learned nothing to inspire critical thought of the establishment or Empire at the time that it was being shed of its major territories. Anti-imperial resistance in Kenya, 'British Guiana', Cyprus or Malaya was caricatured as the work of savages or communists, and even the images on television screens of the Sharpeville massacre or the capture and humiliation of Patrice Lumumba in the Congo seemed to lead to few questions within our suburban studies. The trial in Israel of the Nazi mass-murderer Adolf Eichmann provoked some ripples, and it may have been around then that one isolated incident happened in an English lesson that provoked some of us to think suddenly about what we were learning – and about the impact it might have upon those not quite fully included within our cultural conformity.

As part of our GSE O-level syllabus for English Literature, we had to read a selection of early English ballads from *The Oxford Book of Narrative Verse*. These included 'border' ballads such as 'Jock o' the Side', 'Sir Patrick Spens' and 'Hugh of Lincoln and the Jew's Daughter'. Our English teacher read these out loud to us with a strong expression and an assumed 'border' accent. We were reading 'Hugh of Lincoln', and had reached the stanzas where the Jew's daughter, having lured the young aristocrat into her house and prepared him for a living sacrifice, proceeds to deliver the final blow. The teacher read on, deeply involved with the poetic language:

> She's wyled him in through ae dark door,
> And sae she has through nine;
> She's laid him on a dressing table
> And stickit him like a swine.

And first came out the thick, thick blood
And syne came out the thin,
And syne came out the bonny heart's blood;
There was no more within.[5]

The horrific effectiveness of the poetry touched all of us. No-one more so than Anita, the one Jewish student in the class, who, shocked, shaken and repulsed by the poem, began to weep, her head in her hands, and then ran from the classroom in distress. Suddenly we understood why, and we realised the power in language and knowledge that could cause such pain. Anita's friends went after her and comforted her. Although at that time no-one who was there would have identified a curriculum of racism and exclusion in the teaching of this poem (for a national public examination purpose too), that is what it was. For there can scarcely be a more brilliantly-composed racist poem in the English language than 'Hugh of Lincoln and the Jew's Daughter', and we were using it to pass our GCSE O-level English literature.

I write of these things because they illustrate the intense systems of social polarisation and exclusion in structure and curriculum that were the bedrock of the British education system before the introduction of comprehensive schools. Not that their gradual and uneven implementation across Britain ended that subliminal reality of educational exclusion, but they have challenged and undermined it in many different contexts and situations.

A LONDON CLASSROOM

I returned to school as a London teacher at the turn of the 1960s, after teaching in Canada and the Caribbean. My own experiences in education had made me a strong supporter of comprehensive education. I began to teach English at a school in east London which deemed itself to be comprehensive despite its connection to a Church of England foundation, but soon discovered that it was only nominally so, like hundreds of others. It was rigidly streamed, with its lowest stream in each year (called the 'remedial' class) having thirty students in it, many of whom were barely literate. There were also three 'voluntary-aided' grammar schools within a mile of the school (one in the next street), which 'creamed off' from local working-class neighbourhoods some of their sharpest and most motivated young people. Institutionalised polarisation and exclusion were fundamental. I found it absurd that schools calling themselves 'comprehensive' could be streamed. With such violent categorisation and separation by so-called 'ability', such schools were little more than large institutions that put grammar school and secondary modern schools together as one structure, without creating the genuine amalgam of learning, choice and opportunity that formed the basis of the comprehensive school strategy and the principle described by Benn and Chitty as 'giving equal value to all learners and all forms of learning'. Such a principle, I believed even then, was essential to comprehensives – and to what I was later to know as 'inclusive education'.

My own approaches to education led me into constant conflict with the management of this particular school, which I have documented elsewhere.[6] Having already developed a perspective upon internationalism and antiracism in education, I was amazed to encounter such a narrow curriculum in one of the most cosmopolitan parts of Britain – in a school which served a neighbourhood known to be a point of settlement for arrivant peoples from the other parts of Europe, Africa, Asia and the Americas for many generations. As increasing numbers of Bengalis were settling in Whitechapel and Spitalfields, with many of their children entering the school – communities which were vibrant with the excitement of the struggle for the independence of Bangladesh – there seemed little appetite within the school to reach out to them. Even the attempts I made to publish an anthology of the students' own poetry which reflected directly and critically upon the neighbourhood of the school, were treated by its management with suspicion and outright hostility. Thus a curriculum emphasis upon both the local and international seemed to be excluded in favour of a traditional, middle class, quasi-grammar school curriculum being imposed upon an increasingly internationalist cohort of working class children. From the 'banned' anthology, there were voices speaking critically about school, as if their exclusion from its organisation, purposes and practices were a daily experience. These were the poems of fifteen-year-olds, studying for their critical GCE examinations, trying to make sense of their education; but finding little more than boredom and alienation. Sandra wrote:

> We're to sit and work
> All day long we sit.
> The pips go. We rise.
> We leave. All regulated
>
> Step out of place,
> We get told off.
> 'Wear school uniform,
> Wear flesh-coloured tights.'
> It's sickening how these things go
> They never know what we think ...[7]

And who were this 'they'? What was this apparently blind

power which controlled their education? And if education were not about what's true, what is real, what is it about?

> *Them*
> They don't want truth
> They don't want a truthful person
> They must have it their way
> They are the authorities
> We're nothing, just students
> We must do as they say
> They make the rules
> We are forced to obey
>
> *Intiaz Malek*

Reading Susan's *Going to School* now, over a quarter of a century after it was written and published, brings me back to William Blake's *School Boy*:

> Going to school is hard,
> it takes me all day to get up
> out of the warmness
> and to out into the coldness.
> I think of the lessons ahead of me,
> and then I think of the teachers.
> You get freedom out of school
> And you get locked up in school
> just like a prison.
> The bell goes at ten to nine,
> Five more minutes of freedom –
> The bell has gone and I am bored.

The last line of Susan's poem has haunted me ever since I published it in *Stepney Words*, for it seemed to crystallise a process of education that excludes its learners from its very reality. The lucidity and nakedness of all these poems made me think deeply about school and the terrible waste of time it constituted for the young people who were bored and alienated by it – often despite the best and most committed efforts of their teachers. At the heart of this wastage was the examination treadmill, which so many of these teenagers recognised and resisted, despite knowing how vital its processes and results would be for them and their futures. In their insights they seemed to understand how their teachers too were trapped and excluded from the power they merely fronted and mediated. Lorraine, for example, quietly observed in her classes, and given the opportunity, set down these words:

> *School*
> The middle of the longest term of the year,
> All work, all work.
> The teachers have started to get fed up,
> The screams and shouts are getting too much.
> And I sit here staring into space
> Not listening to a word that's said.
>
> The middle of the term, so work must be done
> For the exams that come near the end.
> Everything we have learned is being
> learned to us again,
> And I sit here staring into space
> While the day goes by and by
>
> The teachers are getting restless now.
> Why will the children not learn?
> They just sit here and scream and shout,

They think it's a waste of time.
But it is the profession they choose
So shouting and screaming must be suffered.
So they must keep on.
They must keep on speaking their knowledge
  all day,
Because the pupils must be learned
For the exam that comes at the end of
the year.

The intensity of these feelings of alienation meant that many of these intelligent young people, with all their frustrated brain-power, could not wait to leave what they saw as the mental agony of school and school culture. They showed me that exclusion was as much a state of mind as a state of body – that when they wrote about their classroom being 'dim and dull' or when 'the writing on the blackboard seems smeary, blank', they were saying how intensely they felt they were outside the mainstream of school life. They were saying from the heart of the classroom that they weren't really there. Many of them took their own routes to leaving school as soon as possible, choosing to self-exclude, rather than challenging the school to force exclusion upon them. They would silently disappear from the system though indefinite truancy during the last months of their school lives, and often little was done to urge them to return.

RESISTING EXCLUSION
From the late 1960s, alongside the expansion of comprehensive schools, a range of critical ideas and practices were developing within education, often as a result of community intervention. Many of the initiatives from this period were rolled back during the years of Conservative government,

but some very significant developments took place, some of which are still important. This is particularly true of the many black initiatives against exclusionary practices. Black families and communities were on many occasions a prime focus of resistance to exclusion, and a clear link can be seen between developments inside the school and within black politics more generally.

In 1971, the Caribbean Education and Community Workers' Association, in conjunction with John La Rose's New Beacon Books, published a work of community-led scholarship by Grenadian teacher and researcher, Bernard Coard, *How the West Indian child is made educationally sub-normal in the British School System*.[8] This exposed the reality of large and disproportionate numbers of Caribbean youth being removed from mainstream schooling and put into schools for the then so-called 'educationally sub-normal' (ESN). This was an example of black parents and communities using their own research to intervene in the school system on behalf of their own children, defending them from victimisation and attack through school exclusion.

Coard's book symbolised the determination of black parents and their children not to be rejected or marginalised, and defended the interests of all British children, both black and white, who were being excluded from mainstream education. ESN schools gradually disappeared from the state system (albeit often to be replaced by more cosmetic labels). Significant progress had been made and much encouragement generated, and similar campaigns continued throughout the 1970s and 1980s. In 1985, the black press exposed the fact that black children in general were, as the *Caribbean Times* reported, six times more likely to be suspended from schools than other pupils.[9] In Nottingham, the black community organisation, the UKAIDI Community Link Project, uncovered scandalous levels of school exclusions [10] among African-Caribbean students, and similar community research was conducted in the other cities, with comparable findings. Inner-city black communities were mobilising themselves with democratic scholarship and action long before academics and university education departments began to take an interest in exclusions. In Reading, the Black Parents Action Group were organising, in Bristol it was the Campaign Against Racism in Education, and in the London Borough of Brent, the Parents' Association for Educational Advance. In Sheffield, SADACCA (Sheffield and District African-Caribbean Association) pressurised the LEA to undertake research into exclusions. The results confirmed on a local basis the national picture of a gross over-representation of black students. All this activity was vital in preventing the demonising of black school students. By drawing attention to the injustice of the disproportionate exclusion rate for black children, LEAs were compelled to adopt antiracist policies, remedial measures and fuller ethnic monitoring.

But some teacher unions, in particular the NASUWT, were beginning to resort to other strategies. These were concerned not with tackling the causes and provocations of racism but rather with targeting and blaming the children that were its victims. Pauline Stewart, a courageous black mother, publicly exposed their strategy when she campaigned against the NASUWT's treatment of her son Isa, a 10-year-old pupil at Westminster Junior School in Handsworth. Isa was instructed by teachers at his school to sit alone outside the head's office for two weeks while NASUWT members at the school refused to teach him. Pauline Stewart demonstrated outside the school with Isa and 30 other parents from the African People's Education Group (APEG), holding up placards which declared: 'I have a right to be in school' and

'Justice must not appear to be done it must be seen to be done'. As had happened in other more publicised cases in 1996, Isa had won his appeal against permanent exclusion and the NASUWT were refusing to accept the decision. Having had recourse to her democratic right of appeal and won through, Ms Stewart told the *Times Educational Supplement*, 'What they are doing is unfair. I want him back in the classroom where he belongs. We won our appeal fair and square. The authority (LEA) said the school must take him back but it is refusing to do so'.[11] Pauline and Isa emerged determined victors in this case. Isa stayed in the school and was offered extra support through an additional member of staff.

The brave defence of Pauline and Isa Stewart could be immediately traced back to the inner-city rebellions of 1981 in Brixton in London, Handsworth in Birmingham, Toxteth in Liverpool and Pitsmoor in Sheffield, as well as in other urban neighbourhoods throughout Britain. But such resistance had also manifested itself in less well-publicised forms in many an English classroom during the decade before. In 1972 I found myself working in a Brixton primary school as a 'floating' teacher, attached to a class of ten and eleven year olds. The school served a run-down council estate, just east of Acre Lane, and the children were predominantly from Jamaican families. One morning the white middle-aged colleague who was the class teacher entered the classroom in a grumpy and contemptuous humour, and began to berate some of the children, casting oblique aspersions on their class and race. The class listened morosely, until one large Jamaican boy climbed onto his table and began to chant:

Black is power, white is flour!
Black is power, white is flour!

Another joined him from an adjacent table, then another, and another. Then a white girl did the same, followed by her friend. Very soon the entire classroom, black and white, including those at the table where I was sitting and marvelling at their audacity, were on their feet, on their tables, in unison with the defiant words. The teacher shouted, railed, then gave up and, humiliatingly, walked from the classroom to summon the head. When she arrived, the children were already back in their seats. Their demonstration was over. They had done what was necessary.

Nearly a decade after these events, that same generation of black primary school children, now young adults, took to the streets with the same determination, often with their white working-class companions. In the years that followed, as they became parents themselves, like Pauline Stewart they brought that expression of defiance back to the schools of their own children and 'an end to exclusion' formed the content of many a protest cry.

By the mid-1970s, things were on the move in many London schools, as power changed hands in the Inner London Education Authority (ILEA), and radical policies were established, to make its schools more community-oriented, inclusive and imbued with commitment towards antiracism and antisexism. During the late 1970s and through the 1980s many schools and their teachers took these ideas very seriously and built new strategies based upon them, for use both inside and outside the classroom. 'Sex, race and class' were no longer taboo subjects within the curriculum and the ILEA positively encouraged curriculum development around these themes.[12] A 'multi-ethnic education' inspectorate was established to oversee progress towards multicultural and antiracist education, and well resourced curriculum centres were established throughout London to encourage teachers to use the materials that would help them to become genuine classroom discoverers and scholars who could deal with previously untapped topics and areas of knowledge. The Centre for Urban Educational Studies (CUES), the Afro-Caribbean Resource Centre and the English Centre were three sources that were mined by London's teachers to find the texts and materials they needed. In curriculum terms this was an era of inclusive emphasis. The languages, faiths, histories, music and literatures of London's hugely diverse population were being acknowledged, learned, taught and celebrated in many London classrooms, often in the face of considerable resistance from conservative parents, teachers and politicians. The approach was the antithesis of prescription or an adherence to a narrow 'national' curriculum. Perhaps it is only now, when we measure the straitened limits of the present imposed curriculum on all schools across the country, that we can fully realise the achievement of the ILEA and its teachers during those years.

Teachers were charged and trusted with the fundamental and vital responsibility of curriculum development: to *create* a knowledge base in the classroom which would truly include and reflect the real and diverse lives and cultures of *all* their students. 'Create' because that was what was expected of them and that was what many came to expect of themselves. The notion of simply receiving and 'delivering' approved lesson plans from a centralised curriculum authority – as now demanded by government – would have been seen as anathema by many teachers in London and other British cities during those years. They would have seen it as insulting, as a recipe for a formulaic, lifeless curriculum across schools and classrooms that were seeking originality, creativity and a readiness to respond to the local and immediate needs of the very different communities which each inner-city school served. These teachers felt that they were learning from their students and the communities to which they belonged. Their schools were keen to foster 'community languages' – the students' mother tongues: Bengali or Greek, Caribbean Creole vernaculars or Chinese, Urdu and the languages of West Africa – and the bilingual texts which supported them. Key works of research like the Linguistic Minorities Project's *The Other Languages of England* were compiled as, at last, official recognition and encouragement (sometimes with financial assistance) was offered to the Community Language Schools and Supplementary Classes which black communities had run on a shoestring voluntary basis for years. Community language teachers began to be employed in many urban schools, as funding was squeezed out of the Home Office through Section 11 of the Local Government Act, allowing extra moneys to employ bilingual teachers. As a result, more black teachers entered the system, but many were ghettoised within Section 11 funded posts, with only a few moving into mainstream teaching positions. This influx changed the culture in some schools, creating more understanding and respect for a multilingual and multi-faith culture.

Outside the classroom, in the pastoral and community functions of school, more importance was given to those posts which sought to support students and resolve their own particular social and personal problems and frustrations. New posts were also created which had a community liaison function, seeking to mobilise greater involvement of multi-lingual working class communities in school life. In governance too, other attempts were made to recruit new school governors from black and working-class constituencies in the inner cities. There were seminars and conferences on issues of antiracism, community involvement and the whole range of curriculum issues around languages, history and culture which formed the diverse strands of what the ILEA called 'multi-ethnic education'.

Although the controlling politicians and bureaucrats of the ILEA were often cautious and reluctant to let this new curriculum and community education go 'too far', it had the support of large numbers of parents, teachers, school governors – and the students themselves, who were at last being encouraged through non-examination modules and continuous assessment approaches to find a route into their own communities, languages, histories and literature. The Afro-Caribbean Resource Centre, for example, organised a successful 'Black Penmanship' competition for budding creative writers, the English Centre produced plays, stories, anthologies and memoirs written by London children, which were published professionally, giving a sense of pride and achievement to previously marginalised communities. Videos, tapes and bilingual texts were produced to support the new classroom work. Teachers were given the opportunities for exchanges with teachers in the Caribbean, Africa and the Asian countries of origin of London communities. In some schools, the curriculum began to cut loose from its 'national' moorings and to embrace a more internationalist content – and although the tabloid press marshalled a co-ordinated campaign against such 'multicultural' strategies, with the *Sun* leading the way with its crude caricaturing, [13] there was significant progress towards an inclusive system of curriculum development which genuinely reflected the changing population of inner city schools.

Such developments were bound to be targeted by the Conservative government when it came to power in 1979, led by ex-Secretary of State for Education Margaret Thatcher. Education was a key area of ideological attack for the incoming government, and plans were soon laid for the abolition of the Inner London Education Authority, described by Brian Simon as 'perhaps the largest and most experienced education authority in the world'; [14] the government instituted what even the establishment *Times Education Supplement* called a 'sordid vendetta' against the ILEA's achievements. As the framework was being put in place for the 1988 Education Reform Act and its accompanying 'National Curriculum', it became clear that many of the moves towards a more inclusive national education framework – which had often been set in motion by the ILEA – were to be arbitrarily curtailed. The ILEA itself was duly abolished by the Thatcher government as part of the 1988 Act.

REFERENCES

1. Caroline Benn and Clyde Chitty, *Thirty Years On*, David Furton Publishers, London 1996.
2. See article by Clyde Chitty, 'Selection Fever' in *Guardian Education*, 13.10.98.
3. *Tribune*, 30.10.98.
4. Chris Searle (ed), *Fire Words*, Jonathan Cape, London 1972.
5. 'Hugh of Lincoln and the Jew's Daughter' from *The Oxford Book of Narrative Verse*, Oxford University Press, 1960.
6. Chris Searle, *None but Our Words*, Open University Press, Buckingham 1998.
7. This, and following extracts from Chris Searle (ed) *Stepney Words*, Reality Press, London 1971.
8. Bernard Coard, *How the West Indian Child is Made Educationally Sub-normal in the British School System*, New Beacon Books, London 1970.
9. *Caribbean Times*, 8.3.85.
10. Ukaidi Community Link Project, *Suspensions and the Black Child*, Nottingham 1984.

11. *Times Educational Supplement*, 21.5.93.
12. See pamphlets on *Sex, Race and Class*, Inner London Education Authority, London 1982.
13. Chris Searle, *Your Daily Dose: Racism and The Sun*, Campaign for Press and Broadcasting Freedom, London 1990.
14. Brian Simon, *What Future for Education?*, Lawrence and Wishart, London 1992.

CHAPTER 2

Exclusion and a Headteacher
An Autobiographical Case Study

When I took up my post as headteacher of Earl Marshal School, a comprehensive in north-east Sheffield which served the families of ex-steelworkers and, in particular the arrivant peoples of Pakistan, Yemen, the Caribbean and Somalia, I carried inside me all I had learned about exclusion in education from my own schooldays and my years of working as a teacher in London, Africa and the Caribbean. I had felt the yearning for education of the huge majority of Mozambicans who were denied by the legacy of colonialism the resources to provide a full state education. I had also seen the appetite for knowledge of the thousands who were admitted to school for the first time through the energy and commitment of the new Frelimo government following independence in 1975. While teaching in Trinidad and Tobago in the late sixties I had seen how the exported and life-deciding eleven-plus examination – called in the Caribbean the 'common entrance' – consigned the majority of young people to a desultory continuance of elementary education, while plucking a minority out to enjoy the benefits of a selective 'grammar school' experience. I remembered the rigid streaming of some London schools and my own 'remove' experience. And I cast my mind back to the foundations of all these experiences, my time with my secondary modern classmates, recalling their frustrated and excluded brain power which the British system had never respected. All this to me represented 'exclusion' in education, and with this small area of power which I had achieved as a headteacher, I was determined that exclusion would not be re-visited on the students and communities of the school I now led.

I found no distinction between 'inclusive education' and comprehensive education. I had always envisaged a comprehensive school as one which took and welcomed every child from its neighbourhood or catchment area. And having taken them in, it sought to keep them in through all circumstances, working with them to achieve all dimensions of human development and achievement. As Sivanandan was to put it years later in the preface of my book, *Living Community, Living School*, I felt that I was teaching to elicit 'every conceivable possibility of the human mind and soul', for children were indeed the 'measure of our possibilities'. But all our children. Not only those hand-picked, selected, separated out and installed in privileged schools, leaving the rest excluded and dropped back into nondescript, demotivating and ill-resourced educational experiences. To me exclusion of any kind should play no part in the life of a comprehensive school. The school itself and its reason for being there were to negate exclusion and exclusivity.

During the 1970s in our east London school, we, the teachers, would scout the streets, billiard halls and markets of Poplar searching for truanting students to bring them back to our classrooms. To remove or exclude even the most difficult, troublesome or demotivated students from our school we saw as not just an admission of institutional failure but as human betrayal – an act of denial of the fundamental right of a child for which teachers like ourselves in previous generations had organised and campaigned. It was there, clear and unambiguous in Article 26 of the UN Declaration of Human Rights and the Rights of the Child: that every child had the right to a free, compulsory education alongside his or her peers in a state school – an education that 'promoted understanding, tolerance and friendship among all nations, racial or religious groups'. Britain had been among the first nations to pledge to address that basic need. How could we betray it by excluding our students from the very schools which served and belonged to their own communities? Such a principle underpinned our professional lives as young teachers in London just as the Hippocratic Oath underlined the commitment of doctors. It could not be set aside, even in the most pernicious of market systems.

MARKET DAYS IN EDUCATION

By the time I began as headteacher at Earl Marshal School in 1990, that market system had become strongly institutionalised, even in erstwhile progressive local education authorities like Sheffield. The fourth largest city in England, its LEA had been the first to abolish grammar schools, declare all its schools co-educational and non-uniform and establish a system of comprehensive education and catchment areas across its length and breadth. It gave generous 'positive action' funding to schools in disadvantaged areas (Earl Marshal's catchment area being at the top of its index of disadvantage), which created the scope for extra staffing and resources to meet some of the dire needs of a struggling inner-city school. Section 11 moneys offered the opportunity to employ extra teachers of English as an Additional Language, Community Liaison, African-Caribbean support and – if used creatively – community languages such as Arabic and Panjabi.

However, by 1990, as a direct result of the 1988 Education Reform Act, a market system of education was now operating across British cities. Opportunities for any effective level of 'positive action' funding were suddenly and drastically diminished as funding for schools became based upon undifferentiated pupil numbers rather than pupil needs. Catchment areas were abolished in favour of an open enrolment system, which encouraged many parents to send their children to schools miles away from their homes, and seek out the 'prestige' institutions in middle-class neighbourhoods where they believed their children would have a greater level of academic success. Inner-city schools like Earl Marshal began to lose their students, and with declining student rolls came increasing material impoverishment, and the loss of teachers and resources. An ever-accelerating spiral of decline for inner-city education was set in motion, while more and more power was removed from progressive LEAs which had looked after and funnelled extra resources towards those schools in working-class areas with the most acute needs. Some of the students who lived in working-class neighbourhoods but were despatched to suburban schools grew alienated or disaffected in their 'long distance schools' and would get into trouble, be excluded or expelled. Then their parents would seek admission for them to their local schools, which they had initially leap-frogged. It was a common pattern, and meant that schools like Earl Marshal would be asked to admit large and disproportionate numbers of excluded students. We always welcomed them, pleased to offer them another chance in their local school, which we felt was, in any case, their true educational home. When it became known across the city that we were admitting students whom no other school would consider – sometimes because of a one-off involvement in drugs or violent behaviour – excluded students from outside our communities sought admission. And rather than seeing them consigned to the streets, we admitted them too, so long as their parents would give assurances of their support and continuing involvement.

But more of this later. Earl Marshal was prepared to defy the consequences of the market system of schooling by remaining as loyal as possible to the principles of comprehensive, inclusive and community education. As the composition of its governing body changed to reflect the true composition of the community it served with strong representation from local Pakistani, Somali, Yemeni, Caribbean and local white communities, there was for the first time a Sheffield comprehensive with a black chair of governors and black majority membership supported by white colleagues who also had firm commitment to comprehensive, antiracist and community education principles. Now the governance of the school began truly to represent the 85 per cent school student body from local black communities. Since it was these communities which had suffered most grossly and unfairly from permanent exclusions across Sheffield (as in other cities such as Birmingham, Nottingham, Bristol and most of the London boroughs), this strong governing body naturally supported a policy which discouraged any form of exclusion within the school, and expressly declared its opposition to permanent exclusions. Thus was created the 'notorious' (or 'commendable', depending on your point of view) Earl Marshal 'non-exclusion policy', agreed and upheld by the school's governors and headteacher.

A 'NON-EXCLUSION' POLICY
As a policy document there was nothing unique about it. It

reserved the right for governors to finally exclude if they felt every possible alternative had been exhausted. That right was invoked in only one case over five years, when an irate boy punched a teacher in the face after another teacher (whom the injured teacher was protecting) had pulled his dreadlocks while the boy was involved in a scuffle with a classmate. Even in this case the excluded boy had more than an element of justification on his side. But the significance of the governors' commitment against permanently excluding students was in their practice rather than in their policy making. As they were mainly local residents, they knew well the dangers that faced young people who were refusing to go to school, absenting themselves from it through truancy or self-exclusion, or had been propelled from it through formal exclusion as a sanction. Thus when they approved the wording quoted below, they knew precisely what risks were faced by those young people who were out of school. Firstly, as the mainspring of their policy, they agreed:

> The policy of the school is not to use exclusion as a routine disciplinary approach in any area of school life. Exclusions from lessons as well as exclusions from school will be discouraged. The approach of the school is to *resolve* its problems internally, to find creative and lasting solutions to any behaviour that interferes with the normal operation of school life.
>
> Permanent exclusion from school will only be invoked in an extreme or unresolvable situation, after every other possible expedient or sanction has been exhausted. The school will always seek to use the invaluable resources of the community through parental involvement, governor involvement and the support of community groups and associations to seek solutions to problems of student indiscipline.

Words only. But what was the reality which faced their sons and daughters if they found themselves excluded from school? The prevailing dangers were strongly set down in the writings of the students, published by the school in a series of poetry anthologies, including one called *Heart of Sheffield*, where the writers expressed the contradictions of their neighbourhoods. The viciousness of much of the crime contrasted starkly with the humour, friendliness and good neighbourliness that was to be found in abundance too. A thirteen-year-old Somali boy described the estate next to the school:

The place I live in is called Wensley Street.
There's lots of bad things happen there
Joyriders smashing cars up,
Always cops trying to arrest someone
And the person is running away.
There's a lot of burglars every day
and someone breaking into someone else's house.
No-one's doing anything about it
Because they're scared that if they snitch
They might get beaten up
Sometimes Wensley's not so bad
Children playing on the field, shouting,
'We won!'
'We beat them!'
'We played better!'
On the football pitch, big and large
Or neighbours being friendly,
Saying nice things to each other
And always laughing![1]

Yassien Yusuf

The school was in the centre of one of the most crime-laden parts of the city. Almost every Monday morning would dawn to a fresh burnt-out car wreck on the unfenced school campus, to be passed by the students as they came to school. The dangers of local crime – burglary, drug-trafficking, joyriding, car theft and the torching of robbed vehicles to destroy fingerprints – were strongly impressed upon the minds of the students. Exclusion in real terms meant throwing a teenager directly into that world, into the daytime streets where crime was often most rampant, either as protagonist or, in this case, as victim:

> *Panic*
> I was walking back from school
> I saw a boy with a brick.
> All I could do was panic and run.
> He caught up with me and stripped me –
> Panic! Panic! Panic!
> I was very scared.
> He said: 'Give me your money!'
> I said I never had any
> So he put the brick to my neck.
> Panic! Panic! Panic!
>
> *Deana Elvin*

Each one of these poems was a convincing reason not to exclude students from school and set them down aimlessly on the street, in real jeopardy of being sucked into crime and violence. But the same neighbourhoods were also redolent with a drug culture, which was an active menace to their young people. And the physical evidence was frequently found on the school grounds – empty receptacles and disused syringes, and certain houses and cafés within easy distance of the school campus were well-known as centres of drug use and commerce. For Shama, the story of a used syringe picked up by a toddler as his mother walked him over the waste ground near the school, was what set her words working:

> *The Needle*
> The needle
> that was lying on the floor.
> The needle
> that was calling me more and more.
> The needle
> that shone in my eye
> The needle
> that convinced me
> not to live but to die
> The needle
> that gives me pain
> The needle
> that turns me insane
> The needle
> which will never let me
> be a good wife
> The needle which has taken over
> my life!

Where were the local havens for the truants and the excluded? Shopping malls, the city centre, local derelict houses, dead end streets and cafés stacked with gambling machines and digital games. The writer of this poem was thirteen, a compulsive truant and an even more compulsive gambler. His regular school-hours habitat was a local Yemeni-owned café whose management allowed him to work their machines to addiction level. As he wrote in a rare English lesson:

I went in the café
when I started this school
and I kept going in.
One of my friends
took me into this café
Since then
because of the arcades
playing those machines every day
I can't come back out from it
unless I have no money left.

EXCLUSION AND CONFLICT

The contradictions within the school over exclusion became starkly and typically clear over the case of this Caribbean boy. Whereas some teachers spent much time, energy and commitment tracking him down, trying to keep him in school, motivating him and counselling him, having long discussions with his parents, even physically extracting him from the café on many occasions – in short doing everything possible to hold him in school and persuading him to stay and gain something from the experience – others did just the opposite. They called for his permanent exclusion, sometimes humiliating and provoking him even while his father was in prison and his mother was living in another city. They complained that he was not interested in their lessons, defiant and insubordinate to them in class, and difficult to control and discipline. Their solution was that he should be permanently out of the school through the school's choice, not regularly out through his own. While some teachers were trying to persuade him in, others were intent on putting him out. It was a paradigm that became more and more common within the school. For while the head and governors strongly held the position that it was essential to keep the most demotivated and vulnerable students in school – precisely because of their vulnerability, while resolving to spark their motivation and change their behaviour – the position of certain other teachers was that 'troublemakers' should go, since they made teaching difficult, created an unsafe environment for teachers and other students and interfered with the classroom progress of the majority of serious learners.

They had a point, of course. It took a particular kind of professional commitment to be prepared to work – day in, day out – with difficult and challenging students. Yet my argument was that we were in this school to do just that. If we'd wanted an easier or more comfortable teaching life, we would have chosen a different school in another part of the city. The vibrancy, creativity, humour and enormous talent and brain-power of our students, their potential, the astonishing achievement of their bilingualism – all this was more than compensation for the few difficult students we had resolved to keep teaching and trying to improve their behaviour and attitude to learning. Also, where else as teachers could we learn so much as in a school like Earl Marshal? Here was a true 'school of the world' whose students taught their teachers about new areas of life, language and experience every day, where the internationalism of the ethos meant we learned as much from our students as they learned from us, if we were open to this blaze of knowledge from new cultures, faiths, literatures and histories. The school's essential cosmopolitanism made it a unique learning place – a virtual university in a small neighbourhood in north-eastern Sheffield, for teachers too, if they would only be prepared to acknowledge and benefit from it.

Such arguments meant nothing, sparking little more than derision from those teachers who saw schools as venues of one-way education, of authoritarian teaching and 'bank' learning – or those convinced that education was merely the 'delivery' in the classroom of a prescribed and narrow curriculum, slim and chauvinistic, there to mould a national identity in the face of such broad and massive internationalism as was represented by our students and their families.

In the context of Earl Marshal School, the main internal body of opposition to the no-exclusion policy was organised through the NASUWT. These teachers were reflecting not only their own antipathy to the policy, but also the position of their union leadership, which had long promoted the practice of permanent exclusion for 'disruptive' students. The Union's General Secretary, commenting in response to figures about exclusions being released by the government, declared that far too few 'disruptive' school students had been permanently excluded in schools across the nation. One hundred thousand more should go, he told BBC Breakfast Television on 11 May 1998. Such figures, inordinately high, had been evoked a month before by New Labour Employment Minister Margaret Hodge, who revealed that 250,000 young people across Britain had reached the stage of what she called 'status zero', being out of school yet out of work too, living betwixt and between with no viable profit or value taken from school life.[2]

My own relationship with the NASUWT at the school level had become strained after my first month in the school, when I received a number of sexual harassment complaints about one of their members, both from girl students in the school and some female members of staff. Complaints about him had been made before my arrival at the school, but no action had been taken. When allegations emerged of serious misconduct, with girls revealing that they had been indecently propositioned and touched, I had to suspend this teacher. For all the girls and colleagues concerned it was an upsetting experience, but for several Islamic girls it caused a distress that was almost inconsolable. They could not talk about the experience except to female teachers whom they knew well and trusted, insisting that what they had to say must never reach their parents, for the stigma involved would forever stay with them. They could only write down their stories which revealed reactions of terrible fear and shame. The teacher was represented by his union, which argued that I was exaggerating the incidents (which went back over a number of years) and in a hearing before the members of the local authority successfully pointed to the inconsistencies around the dates and memory in the girls' evidence. Thus, largely through technicalities, the union secured an acquittal for their member – who never returned to the school. It was the worst of beginnings for me as far as the NASUWT was concerned.

I had been an active teacher trade unionist all my professional life, from the first year of teaching in London when my union, the National Union of Teachers (NUT) vigorously defended me, and eventually regained my job for me two years after I had been dismissed in 1971 for publishing my students' poetry in *Stepney Words,* in defiance of the headteacher and governors of the school. I had been helped enormously by a mass protest strike from students in the school, and the support of many people in the community. So I found trade union opposition to my policies and practices in Earl Marshal a difficult and hurtful problem. The school staff was split between membership of the NUT and NASUWT, with the latter having greater numbers and a certain dogged determination, which, over many bread-and-butter issues, I admired. I certainly did not want to be involved in a continuous battle with trade unionists in my own profession, and sought compromise and non-confrontation whenever it was possible. But what astonished and continuously disappointed me was the inclination of the NASUWT membership and its leadership to use its power *against* young people at school – a situation I had not encountered before. I had many times taken trade union action at school level with fellow union members – often in co-operation with the NASUWT, on issues ranging from wage claims and workload protests, to strike action against asbestos in school buildings. But I was shocked by the constant rhetoric and attacks on 'disruptive' children whom, the NASUWT claimed, were the main barrier to progress in schools.

THE COMMUNITY: A RESOURCE AGAINST EXCLUSION

An essential part of the school's approach to dealing with students who were demotivated, unruly or undisciplined was to involve not only their parents – a conventional but essential line of support and intervention – but also the school governors and community associations connected to the school. Some of the governors themselves were active members or officers of the Yemeni Community Association, the Somali Community Association, the Sheffield and District African-Caribbean Association (SADACCA), the Pakistan Muslim Centre or local Pakistani mosques in the neighbourhood of the school. As governors, they became a direct line to these organisations which were connected to the Sheffield Black Community Forum, with which the school also had strong connections. Many of these links had been forged during 1990-91, when the school worked closely with its constituent communities to build a local campaign to save it from the threat of closure by the local educational authority.[3] Since so many young black people were becoming the victims of school exclusion, and since a 1985 LEA survey provoked by the protest of Sheffield's black communities had shown that Earl Marshal, along with other schools in Sheffield, excluded a disproportionate number of black students, these community associations were strongly supportive of the new 'no permanent exclusions' approach and were keen to help make it successful. 'Exclusion ruins young lives!' declared the chair of governors at a conference on the topic. And it was this theme of young people in jeopardy, having been cast out of school that was the foundation of these communities' humane opposition to exclusion.

As headteacher, I was not opposed to 'overnight' exclusions, or temporary exclusions for three days for a serious or violent offence to give time for reflection and cooling down. Such brief exclusions were often a direct incentive to provoke the involvement of reluctant parents, or those who had little contact with the school. What the governors and I opposed was the use of *permanent* exclusion, the removal of students from the school when they needed help, counsel, structures for self-discipline and consistent support for changing their ways and developing their character. Exclusion would only make their behaviour worse, as they became prey to all the dangerous daytime influences at large in the school neighbourhood. We had support from many local shopkeepers and residents and pensioners for our policies. Keeping 'difficult' young people in the school and struggling to change their behaviour was seen locally as one of the prime responsibilities of teachers. The police also supported our efforts, taking the view that the policy made their task easier; it was better for teachers to educate against and prevent crime in school than for the police to deal with it on the streets around the school. It was with some bemusement that I found myself visited by the very attentive Chief Constable of South Yorkshire and invited to the local police station to a meeting to explain the details of our policies and approaches.

During 1990-91, and the following years, many young Somalis joined schools in Sheffield. They arrived directly from escaping the consequences of civil strife in northern Somalia and the government bombardment and repression in their home cities of Burao and Hargeisa. Many of them had experienced terrible events, seeing close family killed before their eyes. Others had been physically involved in military activity, despite their youth, and some bore the bodily and emotional scars. When one of our fifteen-year-old Somali students complained of aches in his leg, he was found by the hospital to have a bullet in it, which later had to be removed. Many of these young people were traumatised twice over, first by the war and journeys of escape over harsh terrain to Ethiopia and then by the racism they encountered in England. Ali's story was not uncommon.

Journey from Burao
I was born in a country called Somalia
in a city called Burao.
Somalia is in East Africa
It is a big country.
Most of the time it's dry
But it's a hot country and a beautiful place
With tall mountains and a lot of grass.
I used to play football with my friends
And used to swim down on the beach on the river.
Then the war started again when I was ten years old;
And I was frightened, it was a bad war.
My Uncle Issa Haq was shot by the soldiers
You could see dead people everywhere,
So we used to stay indoors to be safe –

We might get killed by firing if we went outside.
The worst time was when it got to night-time,
You could hear people screaming all around.
I used to cry every night,
I used to say to myself
'I wish this war would stop
And the government soldiers in their green uniforms
would go away.
And people could live together in peace.'
This was my dream...[4]

Many students told of their long wait in Ethiopian refugee camps, of the struggle for visas and the right to join relatives in England. Abdi wrote:

> It took a whole year to reach here,
> We went to so many places in between
> So many places in Africa
> Where we had to move from place to
> place...

And Ali added:

We passed a lot of people riding donkeys
We passed through Diredawa in Ethiopia
We travelled to a city called Addis Ababa.
We lived there for three months in a hotel
And after that we flew to Russia.
We stayed in Moscow for just one night
And most people were sleeping on the floor.
My mother asked if they had a bed for me to sleep on,
She said, 'I have a child, he can't sleep on the floor.'

So they gave us a bed to sleep on;
And the next morning we left Russia.
After eight hours we landed in London Airport,
And a van was waiting for us to take us to Sheffield.
I met a lot of friends here and they taught me
English,
And after a year at school I had learned the language
Now the war is finished I feel like going back to Somalia
To become a doctor and help the people.

But not all these young people were as focused and as clear in intention as Ali. Many young Somalis were confused, unsettled and fragile. As a school, we needed all the help of the local Somali community and its association to help us stabilise these new students. Some of their teachers complained about their attitudes, their occasional petulance or anger. One boy, Yusuf (who had been on the fringe of rebel military activity in Somalia) soon attracted the ire of a small group of teachers who saw him as dangerous, aggressive and disrespectful. There were calls for his exclusion – particularly after he was found carrying a knife to school, and brandishing it at a Pakistani classmate. Radical steps were needed, so we sent him for two days to the Somali Community Centre, where he spent time with his community's leaders, who counselled him determinedly, impressing upon him his responsibilities as one of the first young Somalis of many who would follow, and the need for him to make the most of his education to assure the foundation of a successful life in Britain. When he returned to the school his attitude had changed. He was far more positive, friendly and motivated, and kept away from serious trouble for the rest of his time in school.

This approach of involving local communities, their representative governors and associations became the school's major strategy for avoiding permanent exclusions, and a way of further involving the school's constituent communities in the intimate daily life of the school. When a group of Pakistani boys – led by much older youths who had nothing to do with the school – took to aggressive behaviour and petty vandalism around the campus in the evenings, we mobilised Pakistani governors, the local mosque elders and parents to patrol the school grounds, and to interview and reprimand the boys they found causing trouble in the presence of their parents during the school day. In some cases we asked their fathers to shadow them in school for a day, sitting in on their lessons and closely observing their behaviour. This became a dreaded but occasionally effective alternative to exclusion. Such strategies needed close trust and co-operation with communities and parents. At times they failed, but at other times there was positive change in the behaviour of individuals and groups of students. A girl who was involved in violent bullying was sent to the offices of the Black Community Forum where she was under the eye of the vice-chair of Governors. She not only benefited from the advice and friendship of women workers there, but she also learned some clerical skills and returned feeling very positive about the experience, and aware of how damaging her behaviour had been.

Other approaches to avoid exclusion came from the self-organisation and initiatives of the students themselves. For example, at one point during the winter of 1993-94, serious tension developed between boys from the Pakistani and Somali communities. There was a dangerous drift towards communalism outside the school, and it was beginning to spread internally. Group fights began to take place on the campus during dinner hours and after school, and the situation worsened after an affray at the main bus stop outside the school. Teachers' efforts were proving ineffectual, and although we informed the governors and parents, it was a dangerous situation that only the youth themselves could dispel. Fortunately, some boys and girls from the Yemeni community came forward – a community which itself had experienced the tensions of internal division. For years Yemenis in Sheffield had seen themselves as either from the North and aligned to the Yemen Arab Republic, or from the South and loyal to the socialist republic with its capital in Aden. The 1990 unification of Yemen as one country had been greeted with satisfaction by Sheffield Yemenis who then united to form one community association, and this remained a unified body despite the civil war which broke out in Yemen in 1994. So the young Yemenis knew all about division and internecine conflict.

The Yemeni school students called some influential members from the Pakistani and Somali boys' groups together for a crowded meeting, sitting around the large table in my office. I left them to it. After over two hours of passionate discussions (they could be heard well beyond the office walls) the students emerged, clasping each other's hands and claiming that they had resolved the problems between them. The young Yemenis, with the faraway adults of their country at war, had become the peacemakers in a Yorkshire city on another continent. I could only marvel, for their mature and responsible action – inspired by the insights arising from their own history and present – had prevented a serious situation deteriorating to even more fearful levels. And they had done it themselves. Nobody was excluded, and although there was a residual tension between many of the boys of both communities, the hostility and suspicion gradually dissipated.

Yet many teachers, in particular NASUWT members, were

worried about these developments. To them, it seemed as if the teachers were losing control of the school to the communities that surrounded it, together with the students. The NASUWT group began to urge the permanent exclusion of more students whom they saw as 'unteachable' and out of control. As headteacher, I could see that the conflict was clearly with particular teachers, often those who used authoritarian classroom styles, who relied upon physical presence or clumsy insults and sarcasm, whose classroom performance was apathetic or unenthusiastic or who hinted at, or sometimes openly expressed, racist attitudes. With other teachers these students would behave impeccably, showing friendliness and motivation. Their behaviour was selectively aimed towards particular teachers as a form of conscious resistance, in the same way that some of the same students practised selective self-exclusion, truanting from lessons which they found tedious, oppressive or irrelevant but always being present at the ones they enjoyed. It became clear that much of the students' action had its own rational base.

The situation reached crisis level after one NASUWT member pushed a petulant student against a wall during a lesson, causing the student to push him back. It was not a violent push – the fifteen-year-old Pakistani boy was a talented amateur boxer and if he'd felt inclined he could have responded much more forcibly. But the NASUWT called for immediate exclusion. I had been called to the incident, removed the boy from the classroom, escorted him to my office and telephoned his father – who was a frequent attender of school functions, a helpful supporter of the school and a reasonable and friendly man. He came immediately and was keen to talk to the teacher with the boy present, and so resolve a difficult situation with good will and cooperation. I explained all this to the teacher, who said – on the advice of his union – that he did not wish to meet the parent, who patiently, politely and futilely waited all afternoon in the hope of such a meeting. It could have been a constructive meeting with the most reasonable of fathers, but the teacher and the NASUWT were not interested. They insisted that the boy should be excluded forthwith, and issued a statement that NASUWT members would no longer teach him, or two other students who had been involved in what they defined as unacceptably disruptive behaviour.

The NASUWT members were breaking contract, so in theory I could have taken disciplinary action against them. However, I was also a trade unionist and, although I disagreed fundamentally with the cause of their action, which seemed to me directly aimed against the students and their families as well as the management, I decided not to be confrontational but to seek a solution through persuasion and cooperation. The deputy head or I took the boycotted students when a NASUWT member refused to have them in their class. This was anything but satisfactory, and the students began to miss important examination subjects. Soon their attendance in the school, irregular at the best of times, became still more erratic. Thus the NASUWT began to gain its objective by the students' self-exclusion, and I found myself in the cleftest of cleft sticks.

As far as the NASUWT was concerned, it became clear after this that they wanted me out, and they did everything they could to achieve this. First came low-level internal warfare, such as the complaint one of their members made about me for physical harassment of a student after I had publicly slapped him on the back while congratulating him and presenting him with a certificate of excellence during an assembly. Then there was a letter to the local Member of Parliament and Shadow Secretary of State for Education,

David Blunkett, complaining about my management and the school's policies and inclusive approaches. It was his letter to Sheffield's Director of Education, recommending that I be removed from the school that eventually led a year later to the LEA taking away the delegated powers of the governors – which had the only black majority membership in Sheffield – and then excluding me permanently with the power they had expropriated. But by that time, Blunkett's intervention had triggered two OFSTED inspections within two months during the summer of 1995, and these resulted in the school being put under 'special measures' as a 'failing' institution.[5]

The final irony is that since these events, the New Labour government and its Secretary of State for Education, David Blunkett, have frequently exhorted schools to reduce the numbers of permanent exclusions of students across the nation. They have even recommended that this can be best achieved when schools and local communities are working closely together for the benefit of all their students; using some of the very same strategies that we were pioneering at Earl Marshal.[6]

REFERENCES

1. This poem and those that follow are from *Heart of Sheffield*, Earl Marshal School, Sheffield 1995.

2. Margaret Hodge, MP, speaking on BBC Radio Sheffield, 9 April 1998.

3. See Chris Searle, *Living Community, Living School*, Tufnell Press, London 1997.

4. This poem and those that follow are from *School of the World*, Earl Marshal School, Sheffield 1994.

5. See 'Ofsteded, Blunketted and Permanently Excluded' in Chris Searle, *Living Community, Living School*, as above.

6. *Times Educational Supplement*, 2.10.98.

CHAPTER 3

'Lethal Discourses'
The Exclusive Curriculum

The curriculum of our lives is the sum of what and how we teach and learn in and out of our schools. Because it is the cognitive base for freedom to learn, to create insight and understanding, it is continually vulnerable to capture and prescription by those in power and government. This is what happened when the National Curriculum was introduced in 1988 as a part of the Conservative government's new body of education legislation. Although much of the 1988 Education Act was designed to develop a market system of state schooling (see pp26–7), there was to be no 'market choice' of knowledge in schools. Instead, in the area of curriculum there was the new authoritarianism of an imposed 'command' curriculum. Powerfully centralised, and composed of knowledge approved and licensed by government-controlled educational advisers and quangos, it soon became narrowly prescriptive and prohibitive of classroom knowledge outside of its strongly regulated 'orders'. All this was to be overseen by the regular surveillance of OFSTED school inspections. Although this new curriculum was introduced as a guarantor for 'entitlement', with much emphasis placed upon an assurance of achievement for all, it soon became clear that it would operate as a mechanism for the control and exclusion of knowledge.

A National Foundation for Educational Research project in 1996 found the curriculum to be a major source of disaffection and student turn-off in British Schools,[1] and even research done for the QCA (when it was still called the School Curriculum and Assessment Authority) concluded that the rigid, canonical and culturally narrow English curriculum in our schools was having that effect. It concluded that the SCAA were cold-shouldering the findings and ignoring their own research conclusions.

> Teenagers are being turned off Shakespeare because they have to sit an exam on his work at 14 and that encourages boring teaching and parrot fashion learning, according to the report.
>
> The Schools Curriculum and Assessment Authority (SCAA) commissioned the report. But when the SCAA summed up the report's findings, in a circular to schools, it failed to mention the serious criticism of Shakespeare tests.
>
> Teachers suspect that the SCAA sat on the argument because the Conservative government had made a virtue of its commitment to classic books and traditional examinations.
>
> The teachers are hoping the debate about the curriculum will re-open under Labour, although Education Secretary David Blunkett is unlikely to make any early changes.

This comes from the *Yorkshire Post* (21.5.97), which is not known for its liberal views.

Many teachers initially hoped that the 1997 New Labour government would offer some relief from central prescription, with a retreat from the commandist curriculum which they were compelled to 'deliver' in their classrooms. New Labour's electioneering mantra of 'Education, Education, Education' had seemed to suggest a broad and inclusive approach to all aspects of state education, with essential changes to the straitened curriculum a particular priority. In fact, the Labour government continued the trend towards narrowness and exclusion, and their concept of a 'National Curriculum' moved further and further towards 'curriculum nationalism'.

Under New Labour prescription began to cover methods of teaching, and new controls governed pedagogy as much as content and curriculum. Thus primary teachers were compelled to teach a daily Literacy Hour, with minute-by-minute instructions framed by an emphasis upon whole-class teaching and phonics, which was stated to be, quite exclusively, 'the way' to teach reading. They found, too, that of the eight historical periods chosen for the teaching of history to children between seven and fourteen, seven focused exclusively upon events in Britain.[2] And this was in a social context where many inner-city neighbourhoods have become hugely cosmopolitan over the last three decades, with the number of first languages spoken having greatly increased. For example, in London, the number of different first languages has moved beyond 300, and there are in England 33 communities with more than 10,000 people born outside the country.

With the onset of the National Curriculum, exclusion, already historically endemic in the curriculum of British schools, became even more structured and institutionalised. The lives and experiences of millions of Britain's people form little or no part of the knowledge affirmed and valued in the mandatory curriculum. Not that this is new: working-class life, wisdom and culture has rarely had any mention, let alone any emphasis, within the mainstream curriculum of schools in Britain. In the 1970s and 1980s the progressive teachers' movement had begun an attempt to challenge this exclusivity and a significant number of teachers – supported by major local education authorities like the ILEA – had adopted teaching strategies that took account of the experiences and discourse of the majority of their pupils. But the National Curriculum has smothered most of this by imposing a dominant curriculum ideology of the 'nation'. Exemplified by the specific study of literature, history or language, the curriculum has, to quote the words of Edward Said, been 'bound up with the development of cultural nationalism, whose aim was first to distinguish the national canon, then to maintain its eminence, authority and aesthetic autonomy'.[3]

It is a long way back to Charles Dickens and *Hard Times*, but looking at the approved and government-recommended methods of teaching and the choice of what is taught, its echoes are startling, as we see again 'the inclined plane of little vessels ... then and there arranged in order ready to have imperial gallons of facts poured into them until they were full to the brim.'[4] Dickens' acute pedagogic insights about education, in the century when state education was first introduced in England, are remarkably close to the ideas of literacy educator Paulo Freire of Brazil, who died in 1997. Freire is precise about 'exclusion in the curriculum'.

In a meaningful play on words, he declared that 'reading the world always precedes reading the word and reading the word implies continually reading the world'. He wrote in his *Literacy: Reading the Word and the World*[5] that all learning needs to start from the 'word universe' of the students and their communities:

> the word universe of the people who are learning, expressing their actual language, their anxieties, fears, demands and dreams. Words should be laden with the meaning of the people's existential experience and not of the teacher's experience.

Freire stressed the need for the teacher to chart and understand that universe: 'Surveying the word universe thus gives us the people's words, pregnant with the world, words from the people's reading of the world.'

Freire's conception is both brilliant and basic: as wide as the world and yet as focused as the neighbourhood. He was using the word 'world' in two fundamental ways. Firstly, he was a profound internationalist so the world to him meant its entirety from his own Brazil and its rural and slum areas, to literacy processes in the rest of Latin America such as the Nicaragua Crusade and initiatives in the English-speaking Caribbean, where his pedagogy was – critically – adopted in popular adult literacy processes such as the JAMAL programme in Jamaica or the CPE (Centre for Popular Education) in revolutionary Grenada. Many progressive teachers have since employed and adapted his insights in their teaching in European and North American urban areas. So his view of the world was as wide and huge as the world itself and the multifarious words of all its people.

Secondly, Freire was also a committed localist. There was no contradiction for him here. The world he invokes through the 'word' is also an immediate world of the doorstep – the 'word universe' he speaks of is the community, its schools and its real, dynamic words and languages. The 'cultural' and 'word' universe embraces the smallest of places as well as the largest. And these small community venues all over our cities are, in Freire's words 'cultural universes' that are 'points of departure, enabling students to recognise themselves as possessing a specific and important cultural identity'.

A 'BULLDOG' CURRICULUM
The inner cities of Britain are massive in their internationalism and filled with cheek-by-jowl cultural universes, neighbour-

ing worlds of words and cultures – little universities and universes in their scope, with powerful learning and teaching potential for all who live and work in them. But it is a huge step backwards from the open, boundless learning world of Paulo Freire to the prescribed, tramlined and nation-dominated view of education in the National Curriculum. On the eve of the 1997 general election, Tony Blair, in the *Sun* newspaper,[6] vindicated its view of the English as a 'Bulldog breed', promising, if elected, to 'rouse the bulldog to its former glory'. He also gave emphasis to St George's Day, declaring that it should be 'a day of celebration for English people everywhere'. St George's Day is a day revered by British fascists and ultra-nationalists, but it should be noted that its date, 23 April, is an important day for teachers. It is the anniversary of the death in 1979 of antiracist teacher Blair Peach at the hands of the Metropolitan Police, while he was taking part in a demonstration against the fascist National Front as they marched through Southall, West London.

An expression of this narrow 'bulldog' curriculum also confronted secondary school teachers of English across Britain, as they prepared their lessons and looked for recommended authors and texts to use with their classes. In the Conservative government's official publication outlining the programmes of study and attainment targets for English teachers, *English in the National Curriculum* (HMSO, 1995), there is an entire page of recommended authors for the children aged between eleven and sixteen, studying at Key Stages 3 and 4.[7] Among the sixty or so novelists, poets and dramatists listed, there is not a single black writer – and this was at the end of a decade that saw the Nobel Prize for Literature awarded to three prominent black writers of English – Derek Walcott of St Lucia, Wole Soyinka of Nigeria and Toni Morrison of the USA. But this was also the decade of the institutionalisation of the British National Curriculum; so while international recognition and status for black writers in English has increased, opportunities for studying their works in British schools has diminished.

This is a tragic situation for all children at school, black and white. But for black young people it brings a particular hurt. For what are teachers to say to classes in London, Manchester, Birmingham or Sheffield composed of virtually 100 per cent black students? This exclusion is not simply a cultural lapse: it is injurious and unjust. It also presumes a cultural arrogance that characterises the mindset of the British Empire in its most inglorious days. In 1998, the former Conservative Foreign Secretary, Douglas Hurd, expressed this exclusiveness in an entirely symptomatic way. In his speech before awarding the 1998 Booker Prize for significant fiction in English (there was not a single black writer on the shortlist that year), he asserted that, despite the many 'eddies' and 'currents' of the 'ocean of the English language now in its "floodtide"', there was no doubt that the 'heart of the English novel is in these islands' (meaning the United Kingdom). With these words he was exemplifying the stance of those who formulated the National Curriculum.

In his letters to Guinea-Bissau, Paul Freire wrote words as relevant to our own inner-city young people and their teachers as they were to an emergent African nation breaking free from the cultural bonds of Portuguese colonialism:

> In truth, the process of liberation of a people does not take place in profound and authentic terms unless this people reconquers its own Word, the right to speak it, to 'pronounce' it, and to 'name' the words: to speak the word as a means of liberating their own language through that act from the supremacy of the dominant language of the coloniser.

> The imposition of the language of the coloniser on the colonised is a fundamental condition of colonial domination which also is extended to neo-colonial domination. It is not by chance that the colonisers speak of their own language as 'language' and the language of the colonised as 'dialect'; the superiority and richness of the former is placed over the poverty and inferiority of the latter.
>
> Only the colonisers 'have a history', since the history of the colonised is presumed to have begun with the civilizing presence of the colonisers. Only the colonisers 'have' culture, art and language and are civilised national citizens of the world which 'saves' others. The colonised lacked a history before the 'blessed' efforts of the colonisers. The colonised are uncultured and 'barbarian natives.'
>
> Without the right of self-definition, they are given a profile by the colonisers. They cannot, for this reason, 'name themselves' nor 'name' the world of which they have been robbed.[8]

The National Curriculum commits such robbery by its imposition of an elitist and exclusive canon, both in relation to the international world reflected in Britain's inner cities and in the very local world around each school. Much of the prescribed literature is a stone-dead canon to our students. The recommended books are great works of literature, that should indeed be the property of all, but they are so often not the property of the people who are corralled to read them. Good teachers can make such works speak of their world, but it has not emerged from their students' own streets, their voices, their anxieties, their struggles. It is a curriculum based upon a 'word universe' which is not theirs and from which they have been excluded.

When they see a British inner-city class of fourteen-year-olds, most of whom come from Pakistani, Somali, Yemeni or Caribbean families, confronted with a text from Shakespeare's *A Midsummer Night's Dream* – trying to grapple with a language they have but half-learned, despite the efforts of good teaching to make it all make sense and to reveal its beauty – many teachers find themselves recoiling in rage at the violence of the cultural imposition and the damage done to both the teenage readers and the great dramatist himself. Neither writers nor readers are ready for one another. The readers deserve to express their own lives first. The world of the readers; the school students and their families and communities is where we should be creating and enjoining our text – in the word universe which makes meaning of the process of living, learning and wordmaking. Then words would have real meanings, experience would be included and nourished, not excluded and famished. Freire reminds us that teachers need 'to take the neighbourhood or the street as our own concern, trying to see them and to hear what the people are saying ... we become militants in search of the reality of the area with the people who live there.'

The prescribed voice of the National Curriculum, with its narrow view of language, history and experience, excludes many thousands of inner-city young people; it is the source of tedium, boredom and lack of interest in lessons, and provides the motivation for wide-scale truancy, self-exclusion and underachievement, as well as the disaffection and rebellion which can characterise much of their school life. It is a voice which has come down from empire and domination, an exclusive voice brilliantly recorded in Jamal Mahjoub's novel of the British empire's war against the Sudanese people, *In the Hour of Signs*.[9] In the novel General Gordon's words of martyrdom on the steps of the palace of Khartoum, which have come to be an imperial icon, are reversed as the Sudanese rebels hear that voice exhorting them to forget their insurgency:

> It is a voice they know. It comes from beyond the walls constructed to keep them out, beyond the gardens and the guards. It comes from within and is the same voice which gave them every stillborn child, every sickly goat, every drop of fever, every stony year, every lost son or brother fallen in battle, every league walked, this is the voice that defines and confines them.

OTHER VOICES

Yet in many teachers' experience, when the same young people hear a voice and read the words which affirm, include and excite them, they will take a completely different attitude to language and literature. For example, to see the enthusiastic response of a class of predominantly Pakistani and Yemeni young people to a poem either in their own language by the Urdu writer Faiz or by the Arabic poet of Palestine Mahmoud Darwish, is to see an end to the bemusement and lack of involvement which they show, for example, in response to the land of the fairies and the aristocratic shenanigans of *A Midsummer Night's Dream*. For example, here is a poem by Faiz which I read with a class of fourteen-year-olds:

> *Speak*
> Speak – your lips are free.
> Speak – your tongue is still yours.
> This magnificent body
> Is still yours.
> Speak – your life is still yours'
> Look inside the smithy–

Leaping flames, red-hot iron.
Padlocks open wide
Their jaws.
Chains disintegrate.
Speak – there is little time
But little though it is
It is enough.
Time enough
Before the body perishes –
Before the tongue atrophies.
Speak – truth still lives,
Say what you have
To say.[10]

Faiz's poem caused an explosion of poetry in the class about language itself. Poems of pride in their own voice, their own and their parents' languages – be they, in this case Panjabi, Urdu, Somali and Arabic. A Syrian girl wrote about her Arabic:

My Arabic Language
Words of my language are expressive and dear to me.
That's how I feel about my language.

No matter how far I go
No matter where I am
I'll still think of my precious language.

Some people say that a language
is something that is just spoken.
It is in a way
But there is more to it.
It's something

that is very precious,
It's something
that a person is born with,
It's something
that I would never swap,
It's something that can't be destroyed,
That is all yours and the people around you.
My language
My heart is throbbing
My heart starts to beat more
When my language is mentioned.
I think of me
and what I am going to do.
My language might give me work?
A home?
A good education?

That's what I will always hope for and dream of.
I hope it will come true one day.

Khadeegha Alzouebi [11]

Clearly, these young people, like thousands of others considered to be 'linguistically impoverished', have achieved a highly sophisticated level of learning with regard to the languages that they speak. Bilingual, sometimes speaking three or more languages, they have come to grips with language learning in ways most white suburban children – or their teachers – cannot fathom. They engage in highly complex interactions, translating or interpreting for their parents or grandparents in doctors' surgeries, local council or DSS offices, often dealing with complicated bureaucratic procedures or medical transactions. Yet their brilliance in living within two languages and cultures, their international-ism and learning experience of sojourns in the lands of their origins is frequently viewed in their schools as a disadvantage and in entirely deficit terms. It is discarded as a criterion for formal school success and achievement. Thus is their living knowledge excluded from the mainstream of British educational process. It creates what Toni Morrison in her 1993 Nobel Prize address called 'tongue suicide'. Children in her country, she said, 'have bitten their tongues off and used bullets instead to iterate the void of speechlessness, of disabled and disabling language that adults have abandoned altogether as a device for grappling with meaning, providing guidance or expressing love'. Instead of excluding our students' languages we should be welcoming them, recognising their immense achievement of teenage bilingualism as the equivalent of an A-level for university entry, and incorporating them into our schools as languages of equal value with English and richly motivating word universes.

Thousands of black parents have taken the initiative at local and community level throughout Britain to protect and sustain their languages. Supplementary language classes and schools have been formed in many inner-city areas, administered and staffed by volunteers, often with the most miserly grant aid (if any at all) from LEAs. They hold tenaciously onto and further their languages to ensure that their children have the continued opportunity of their full resources. In Sheffield alone, over thirty community language schools meet on a regular, usually twice-weekly basis, upholding the linguistic wealth of, for example Arabic, Urdu, Somali, Bengali and Chinese.

In classrooms too, school students wage their own individual struggles to forbid the virtual invisibility of their own languages within the National Curriculum. This resistance sometimes gets them into trouble, putting them into conflict with their teachers and propelling them towards the exclusion zone. Such situations can be directly provoked by a youthful determination and obdurateness, that symbolises a will neither to be marginalised nor assimilated by a uniform culture and imposed curriculum that does not speak with the voice of the learner. In the following description of a classroom incident observed in a London school by a young student teacher, Nicholas Bevan, the pupil scorns 'tongue suicide' and risks much to hold on to the dialect and words which she sees as undeniably hers. They will not be taken from her. In this 'confrontation', teacher and pupil are systemically ranged against each other on the 'orders' of a prescribed curriculum, when they should be allies in learning. The one is 'delivering' what she is told by government; the other is holding tightly on to what is hers by right, class and identity. Joanne, the pupil, uses the word 'ain't' in reply to her teacher's question: the teacher 'corrects' her – she should have used 'isn't', the Standard English form. The classroom narrative continues:

> The teacher then went on to try to explain to Joanne the idea of appropriate register and the importance of having standard English as a second dialect; explaining that when she was at home the teacher might say 'ain't' but when she was in school she said 'isn't'. She then gave the example of a job interview and asked Joanne which dialect she would adopt then. Joanne insisted she'd say 'ain't': 'Cos you've got to speak as you speak.' The other students were aware of the question of the suitability of when they should adopt certain dialects, as was Joanne; she was just rebelling against the violence done to her own dialect by the automatic assumption that Standard English was somehow more 'correct' than her own.

The teacher went on to explain that one dialect wasn't 'good' and another 'bad' but that there was a question of propriety. Joanne, however, who showed a great deal of confidence and linguistic awareness obviously felt oppressed by the institutional condemnation of her method of communication and insisted on her own surface structure. She then deliberately went on to transdialectisize much of what she read; a process, which demonstrated great linguistic skill and deliberate bloodymindedness. After this confrontation, Joanne became increasingly more disruptive; rebelling against what she viewed as the imposition of an alien linguistic orthodoxy which naturally assumed her dialect to be somehow 'subsidiary': a corruption. Perhaps this insistence on her own dialect was a pattern of Joanne's response to the societal forces which hypocritically espouse equality whilst in practice saying that you're equal as long as you're equally like them.

Joanne was also of mixed race and I felt that the teacher's correction, essential as it was to follow the tenets of the National Curriculum, was symptomatic of the projection of 'ancilliarity' on to any sections of society divergent from white bourgeois 'standard' culture. However, due to the demands of the curriculum I cannot see how the teacher could have acted any differently.

Later, after a process of cooling down, Joanne read some more and read incidences of 'don't' as 'do not'. The rest of the class corrected her. She then became indignant and said: 'But you told me not to say 'don't'!'

This confident girl was obviously becoming undermined by the 'corrections' that the curriculum demanded that the teacher make, and was becoming unsure and insecure where there had been no linguistic insecurity before the attempt to standardise her dialect. The curriculum had almost denied her expression. It is perhaps little wonder that her behaviour after this point and more especially her curt tone to the teacher necessitated a 'private word' at the end of the lesson. Perhaps it is hard to explain to a child how an institution which shows her no respect is supposed to deserve hers.

The nationalist ethos in the National Curriculum was strongly upheld by Dr Nick Tate, then head of the government's curriculum quango, the Qualifications and Curriculum Authority (QCA); Tate is critical of what he calls 'misapplied cultural egalitarianism' that 'wants to give equal attention to everything'. He prefers that a curriculum should evoke a strong sense of a 'majority culture that is sure of itself'.[12] The National Curriculum becomes an expression of this position, imposed upon every school in the land – and thereby provoking healthy rebellion by progressive and combative teachers and their students.

CHANGE BUT SMALL CHANGE?
Between May and July 1999, the New Labour government organised a review of the National Curriculum, with one of the prior objectives being to create 'a more inclusive curriculum framework'.[13] The Secretary of State's proposals included a reference to the Macpherson Report that followed the public enquiry into the racist murder of south London teenager Stephen Lawrence; he stressed the importance of 'encouraging children to value cultural diversity and ... combating the development of racism'. If teachers thought that this indicated a move away from Dr Tate's emphasis upon the 'majority culture', towards a greater curriculum appreciation of internationalism in knowledge and culture, a new adherence to the multilingual, multifaith, multihistorical realities of British society and a new commitment to antiracism, they were to be disappointed. According to

David Blunkett, Secretary of State for Education, 'We have tended to downplay our culture and we need to reinforce pride in what we have'.[14] There were more echoes of the British Bulldog here, particularly as the process on antiracist education was to be marginalised and sectioned off into a new curriculum area called 'Citizenship'. The Secretary of State's proposals included an assertion of 'the need for mutual respect and understanding' of the 'diverse national, regional, religious and ethnic identities within the UK';[15] but this respect did not extend to permeating the subject studies of the curriculum, and offering an internationalist and antiracist foundation as their cognitive base. Significantly, during the three-month consultation period for these proposals, the Home Office announced that the number of recorded racist attacks in London alone had risen to 7790 victims in the current year, from 1149 during the year before.[16]

The review of the National Curriculum did at last accord some recognition to black writers in English. Although marginalised as 'writers from other cultures', writers such as Soyinka, Walcott, Achebe, Narayan, Desai, Ngugi and Angelou were at least there, and the teachers, examination boards and parents who had campaigned for their inclusion were vindicated. Black British writers, such as Grace Nichols and James Berry and the US writer Mildred Taylor – whose *Roll of Thunder, Hear My Cry* had been a GCSE text ever since the 1970s – were given places on the mainstream supplementary lists for poetry and the novel. It had taken a decade since the introduction of the National Curriculum, but persistence had won through. There was little evidence in the proposals, however, of more emphasis on black or internationalist history, the black contribution to mathematics, Science and Technology and in the Modern Foreign Languages area.

The consultation materials proposed that a non-European language would not count as a 'foundation' or main subject in its own right; but only if it were offered to pupils 'alongside the possibility of studying an official working language of the European Union,[17] Words of Europe would still define the status of world languages – and in fact, would still decide whether or not to permit them to exist on the school curriculum.

The Macpherson Report had been quite unequivocal about the role of schools as key government 'agencies' in stemming racism. It recommended linked action across all phases of school life: 'If racism is to be eradicated there must be specific and co-ordinated action both within the agencies themselves and by society at large, particularly through the school system, from pre-primary school upwards and onwards'.[18]

Yet the report's comments on the curricula of schools could not free themselves from the circumscription of National Curriculum. Although it recommended that 'consideration be given to amendment of the National Curriculum aimed at valuing cultural diversity and preventing racism, in order to better reflect the needs of a diverse society', there was little recognition in the report that the underlying cultural narrowness and chauvinism of the notion of the nation which is at the at the heart of the National Curriculum was itself a major causal factor in the processes of exclusion. While the National Curriculum dominated school life, instead of a much more internationalist, common, broad and inclusive concept of curriculum process and development with the concept of 'nation' removed, the curriculum itself would continue to be a profoundly alienating factor within school life in Britain.

The Macpherson Report charged LEAs and school governors 'to create and implement strategies in their schools to prevent and address racism', but classroom teachers have been given no scope to frame the curricula necessary for this to actually be implemented. Instead, OFSTED, which throughout the first decade of the National Curriculum had a prime role in the stage-by-stage disempowerment of teachers, was to be given a greater profile in the 'examination of the implementation of such strategies'. The recommendations demonstrated that the voice of teachers had been largely missing in the authorship of the report. For it is substantially through the classroom empowerment of teachers over the curriculum, in their essential role as classroom scholars and curriculum developers, that real progress in tackling racism at school can be made.

The record of OFSTED in fostering antiracism in schools is anything but one of achievement and excellence. Many inspectors have demonstrated woeful ignorance and disinclination in offering effective or useful judgement and advice to schools about how to stem racism or educate against it through the curriculum. The two Earl Marshal inspections of 1995 exemplified how hidebound the inspectors were in sticking to a formulaic adherence to the National Curriculum prescriptions, and how fearful they were in stepping away from them. The school was criticised for not stressing the achievement and 'harmony' of the history of the British Empire, with particular condemnation directed against a series of posters which illustrated anti-imperial resistance by peoples of Asia, Africa and the Americas (86 per cent of the school roll was constituted by children from families in those parts of the world). During a discussion with the History inspector who had made these criticisms, I mentioned the work of eminent historians from the Caribbean such as CLR James and Walter Rodney, whose scholarship had emphasised popular resistance against imperialist regimes rather than compliance with them. His answer was monosyllabic and indicated much about the OFSTED level of knowledge and understanding about the curriculum of antiracism. 'Who?' he said. While the curriculum of state schools is controlled and monitored by such ignorance, it is hardly surprising that the end result in the minds of black children should be that four out of ten of them would prefer to attend an all-black school outside state control, where black studies and black history would form an integral part of the curriculum (according to *The Black Child Report*, commissioned by the black research organisation Amenta Marketing). One of the authors of the report issued a pertinent challenge to the controllers of the National Curriculum: 'You either pick this up in the main education system or communities will pick it up and say that our own institutions can do that job'.[19]

The same report gives evidence of the curriculum exclusion that threatens to disenfranchise so many young people. There is also convincing research that shows how the tedium of existing curriculum content causes school student disaffection and boredom – and this in turn leads to disruption, self-exclusion and ultimately exclusion used as a sanction: in other words curriculum exclusion in school can lead directly to physical exclusion from school.

FALSE STANDARDS

The rhetoric of 'standards, standards and standards' – another proclamatory theme of past and present governments, is frequently an authoritarian incentive to yoke inner-city school students to a curriculum which does not speak their voices and renders them invisible in history and culture. It seeks to ignore and undo the vibrant internationalism of British inner-city schools and implant a false and narrow curriculum nationalism in the name of 'standards'. This did not work in the USA and it will fail in Britain too, because young people and their bravest teachers will not accept it. They will wilfully exclude themselves from such a curriculum rather than be excluded by it, which means that the waste – and ofttimes perversion – of brilliant young minds will continue. We should take heed from the report on the US 'Standards Rush' by the Poverty and Race Research Action Council and its conclusions:

> The standards movement further reneges on its promise when states translate standards into curriculum frameworks that reinforce the status quo, elevate certain knowledge to a level of official approval and render poor, African American and Latino students invisible in a curriculum. English/Language Acts standards that call for more reading of 'better' books create an aura of rigour, but if the frameworks fail to address the need for multicultural content, many students will remain on the periphery, perceiving school as another world, another culture.[20]

'On the periphery' is a significant phrase. It echoes the so-called 'peripheral' nations from which the family origins of many inner-city students (in North America and in England) spring. Yet they are the new glory of our cities, their vibrant contribution is transforming much of British urban life, and if encouraged and fostered within a liberatory framework of education, it could transform our schools too. Instead, as Alice Walker writes in her *Anything We Love Can Be Saved*, huge numbers of young people walk excluded along the margins of state education:

> Instead, like plants whose roots are sunk in poisonous soil, we find ourselves producing generation after generation of

blighted fruit. And why is this? It is because the dominant culture, whose values are designed to encourage the full development of the white and the male only – and not even of the disadvantaged of those categories, leaves the rest of us unsupported, except in ways that are frequently injurious to us. It is also because many of us have forgotten or can no longer recognise our own culture at its healthiest. We no longer know that it is the soil we need in order to survive, in order to thrive.[21]

But Walker's sense of optimism emerges also from this analysis. Her hope lies in the culture of the constituent communities that makes up her multiracial America. In our multiracial Britain we need to struggle for a culture that includes all, manifests all and shows a co-operative future to all – not in the narrow, New Labour sense of things 'national' but in the voices and words of all our people, including the young from our multiracial inner cities. As Alice Walker declares: 'They show us the way home, which is the whole earth'.

And 'home' is the local world of our students, beginning from their own word universes, their communities and the ways in which our schools can include, reflect, affirm and value them, giving them confidence and preparing them for the rest of their lives. We should not be casting them aside through cultures of alienation and arrogance – the 'lethal discourses of exclusion, blocking access to cognition' as Toni Morrison called them in her Nobel Prize address.

Morrison's use of the word 'lethal' is not overstated. It provokes reflection upon the increasing number of fatal racist attacks occurring in Britain: the stabbing to death by white youths of black teenager Stephen Lawrence in Eltham, South London; the murder of Ricky Reel, from a Sikh family in West

London, last seen alive escaping from a gang of racist white attackers, his body found hours later in the River Thames; the death of Michael Menson, a young black musician, in 1997 – suffering from severe burns, he told before he died of how he was attacked and set alight by four white youths. What was in the minds of these attackers? What was the racism that drove them to commit such acts? To what extent had their school curriculum and its emphasis on 'national' ends and 'values', left these ideas unchallenged or even bolstered them? Or what of Alison Moore, a young black teacher at Sandhurst Primary School in Catford, south-east London, loved and respected by her colleagues and students, staying late at school to prepare for the next day's lessons, who was attacked by a group of white youths as she left? They shouted at her, abused her for teaching white children, beat her, broke her pelvis, knocked her unconscious, caused severe internal bleeding which meant that she was hospitalised for weeks. What was in their minds? How had they responded to a decade of state education? Could a different model and content of learning have prevented them from acting in the way they did outside Sandhurst School? *The Times Educational Supplement* took up the story:

> Since her discharge from hospital the attacks have switched from violence to intimidation, with a get well card concealing a note threatening the teacher with death if she returned to the job.
>
> Last Friday the 30-year-old was awoken at the home she shares with her six-year-old daughter by the sound of smashing glass. She was confronted by two men in balaclavas who daubed National Front slogans and swastikas on her walls.[22]

Lethal discourses indeed, but accompanied too by words of courage and resistance: 'I am really distressed but equally

I am determined not to let ignorant youths drive me away'.

A resurgence of some old imperial ideas of domination are being carried by this 'National Curriculum', and rather than seeking to counter the effects of an imperial history, such a curriculum only gives it more validity. But the tailored and one-dimensional body of knowledge that it offers is complementing a parallel curriculum being promoted in the mainstream of commercial culture that fills up many spaces in young lives. Films, videos, computer games, and the journals that sustain them, are rampant with a new culture of violence, tyranny and domination, which is opposed by little curriculum power at school to provoke criticism or a counter culture. Recently I encountered a frightening example of this in a game called, simply and unashamedly, *Imperialism*. In a full-page advertisement in the journal *Ultimate PC*, [23] it is described as promoting 'the fine art of conquering the world'. The journal also gave a preview and extensive review of the game, along with another called *Age of Empires* – 'the strategy game of warfare and world domination'. In the preview, the writer declares: 'Everybody wants to rule the world – or so they say – and if they're right, then *Imperialism* is destined to be one of the biggest hits of the year'. The review takes this enthusiasm even further:

> At the heart of *Imperialism* however is a game of epic empire-building, and once you've got your economy rolling, and mastered keeping it there, you'll want to expand. There are 16 lesser nations that you can trade, influence and hopefully take over. The most favoured to (sic) route to global dominance is likely to be a bit of sabre rattling: (sic) establishing a military force to rival the Third Reich and laying into the competition. Get it right and it's a quick route to power ... Sit down for a spell of global domination in the early evening and before you can rub your eyes it's 4 a.m.! [24]

Nothing I have met in many years more blatantly sets out to, as Harold Rosen puts it: 'recruit children to the idea of Empire and attempt to implant its icons and its rituals at the very core of their social memories'.[25]

It is such games that our children are playing, backed up by a 'bulldog' curriculum and a corpus of knowledge stressing nation and exclusivity. The challenge for teachers is awesome, but their most powerful potential allies are there in their classrooms and the streets around their schools. These values can be overturned if we can unite with our students and communities to develop a critical alternative to that curriculum nationalism, cognitive xenophobia and narrow exclusivity which is promoted in schools and government as a common body of knowledge.

REFERENCES

1. Kay Kinder, Alison Wakefield and Anne Wilkin, *Talking Back: Pupils' View on Disaffection,* National Foundation for Educational Research, Slough 1996.
2. *The Times Educational Supplement*, 14 October 1997.
3. Edward Said, *Culture and Imperialism*, Chatto and Windus, London 1993.
4. Charles Dickens, *Hard Times,* Oxford University Press, The World's Classics 1989.
5. Paulo Freire and Donaldo Macedo, *Literacy: Reading the Word and the World,* Routledge, London 1987.
6. *The Sun*, 16.4.97.
7. Department for Education, *English in the National Curriculum.* Her Majesty's Stationary Office 1995.
8. Paulo Freire, *Pedagogy in Process: The Letters to Guinea-Bissau,* Writers and Readers, London 1978.
9. Jamal Mahjoub, *In the Hour of Signs*, Heinemann, London 1997.

10. Chris Searle (ed), *One for Blair*, Young World Books, London 1997.
11. Chris Searle (ed), *Valley of Words,* Earl Marshal School, Sheffield 1992.
12. *Times Education Supplement*, 21.795.
13. *The Review of the National Curriculum in England: The Secretary of State's Proposals*, Qualifications and Curriculum Authority, 1999.
14. CARF No.50, London, July 1999.
15. *The Review of the National Curriculum*, as above.
16. *Metro*, 23.6.99.
17. 'The Review of the National Curriculum in England: The Consultation Materials', Qualifications and Curriculum Authority, 1999.
18. *The Stephen Lawrence Inquiry: Report of an Inquiry by Sir William MacPherson of Cluny*, The Stationary Office Ltd., London 1999.
19. *Guardian*, 27.10.97.
20. Jo-Anne Wilson Keenan and Anne Wheelock, 'The Standards Movement in Education: Will Poor and Minority Students Benefit?', *Poverty and Race*, May/June 1997, Washington.
21. Alice Walker, 'The Sound of Our Own Culture' from *Anything We Love Can Be Saved*, The Women's Press, London 1997.
22. *Times Educational Supplement*, 20.3.98.
23. *Ultimate PC*, October 1997.
24. *Ultimate PC*, November 1997.
25. Harold Rosen, *Speaking from Memory*, Trentham Books London 1998.

CHAPTER 4

'Red Cards, Snatch Squads and Sin Bins' Exclusion and Authoritarianism

The next two chapters move away from an analysis of exclusionary practices within schools to look at the location of these practices within wider public discourses of authoritarianism and moralism. Young people are often a focus for authoritarian anxieties – about falling standards, moral dissolution, crime, the decline into chaos more generally. Thus education can be seen as a means to discipline young people so that they are no longer a threat. And, in pursuing repressive policies within schools, populist politicians can win support from voters for whom the maintenance of public order is a key issue.

In almost all education systems where exclusion has remained a pivotal practice it has been an integral part of fear and authoritarianism. Teachers working in such systems are empowered to warn errant or difficult students: 'Any more of that and you'll be out of here' and similar threats. The threat of exclusion can be as potent as the act itself, and many teachers have long depended upon it to establish their authority in the classroom. At Earl Marshal School, for example, it was the removal of the efficacy of this threat, as well as the removal of the actual sanction, that caused anxiety for some teachers. One of my colleagues once said to me while we discussed our different positions on exclusion, 'but if we can't exclude them, they'll never be afraid of us'; and I remembered similar arguments from two decades before, relating to the abolition of corporal punishment in schools. It seemed that in both situations the key was *fear*, not relevance or meaning. I had learned and taught through years of both brands of sanction, seen the authoritarianism they generated, and wanted no more of it. For with the end of permanent exclusion, a school has to develop a teaching that is based not upon threat but upon consent and motivation. Thus the decision 'to exclude or not to exclude' can become a touchstone for a school and its attitude towards teaching and learning – just as other authoritarian features, such as an insistence upon school uniform or compulsory religious worship, are often symbolic of an oppressive educational ethos. Teachers can often be heard falling back upon received professional wisdom, claiming that exclusion is just common sense. 'It's all we've got left', some declare, as if the end of the pedagogic road has already been reached. I prefer to invoke a sentence of A. Sivanandan, from his preface to a pamphlet on the exclusion of black young people, *Outcast England*.[1] 'Exclusion is seldom the measure of a child's capacity to learn; it is an indication, instead, of the teacher's refusal to be challenged'.

Whenever politicians settle in their rhetoric upon the values of 'common sense', with their words being echoed by the establishment press, then it is time for us to beware. Whether used by Tory or New Labour conservatives, such an invocation invariably provides cover for ideas which will not stand up to critical scrutiny. 'Common sense' as deployed by politicians is almost always an appeal to popular prejudice as a way of refusing to answer well-founded criticism. As

Gramsci knew, the struggle over what constitutes public 'common sense' is a key part of the political process – and an appeal to common sense is part of the process of constructing it. In particular, common sense is often drawn on to argue for ideas and practices which hark back to a better and more orderly time – which of course for the majority of the population never truly existed.

Education is a favoured context for such declarations, and since the education of their children is so precious to parents, such demagoguery is the cause of much anxiety and concern – especially to black and working-class parents, since it is the education of their children which is most often under attack. The press probes and provokes these potential worries, casting itself as the purveyor of the common sense of the nation. The tabloid press in particular, knowing that such diktats arouse alarm and raise circulation, become enthusiastic messengers and endorsers of authoritarian ideas that thrive on anxiety. The confirmation and legitimisation afforded by print seems to render such views right, proper and sound. They come to represent the mainstream of right and sensible-thinking people. What follows is a typical example.

In 1996, when he was Shadow Secretary of State for Education, David Blunkett was reported by the *Daily Mail* as speaking enthusiastically for the reintroduction of school uniforms in 'every secondary school to restore discipline and a sense of pride.'[2] A uniform for school students was no longer a burden or a means of social control, he declared, but 'the salvation of the poor', helping to create 'a culture of learning' and raise academic achievement. People in Sheffield might have found his words confusing, since Sheffield City Council (of which Blunkett was a past leader), had discarded school uniforms for the city's schools, and argued for years that they were irrelevant and even an encumbrance to good learning because they suppressed initiative and inhibited individual creativity.

The *Daily Mail* picked up Blunkett's words with interest – while also acknowledging their true source and inspiration:

> Well, three cheers for him ... even if, this time, Labour really is stealing Tory clothes. Political larceny can be the sincerest form of flattery and, in this instance, most people will consider it no more than sound, old-fashioned sense. For there is now general acknowledgement that the come as you like, do as you please, anything goes ethos of the Sixties played havoc with academic standards.
>
> A smart blazer won't turn a dunce into a swot. That's true. But school uniforms help to create an orderly atmosphere in classrooms where learning can take the place of anarchy.

The key words are all there: 'most people', 'sound, old-fashioned sense', 'havoc', 'anarchy', 'orderly atmosphere' and the conventional myths about the 1960s – which, ironically, were the heyday of school uniforms across almost every school in the country. Here is a smart and fast use of 'spin' language, pulling out all the stereotypes and myths – but it is at its heart dishonest, irrational and cynical. It threatens young people in the way regimental sergeant majors would threaten drafted raw teenage recruits for the first drill of their national military service and it extends the menace to teachers too – for, according to the editorial, 'slovenly children and scruffy teachers are given a stern dressing down' by the New Labour spokesman. The authoritarianism of the past is being dredged up so as to cause the maximum fear of the present. 'Scruffiness' is bad, free choice of clothing is dangerous, rectitude comes with convention, conformity, a repressive and false nostalgia, and children meekly sitting in a classroom and accepting the tidy 'delivery' of the National Curriculum. The narrow gauge of the National Curriculum and the learning of predicted outcomes must be adhered to as the 'standard' and reinforced in all respects, including apparel. It is a convergent discipline from the outside in, from uniform clothes to uniform behaviour to uniform minds – a classic means of social control.

EXCLUSIONS AND 'YOB CULTURE'

Towards the end of 1994, the British press took up the cause of campaigning against 'yob culture' – an expression widely used by then prime minister John Major, and swiftly adopted by journalists and sub-editors as a pretext for hostile profiling of – in the main, working-class and black – youth. *The Times* ran a front-page article headlined 'Expulsions spiral as state schools battle "yobs"'.[3] Their education correspondent wrote of the 'dramatic increase' in exclusions from school as evidence of the 'burgeoning yob culture'. He reported the words of Nigel de Gruchy, general secretary of the NASUWT, who said that 'disruptive pupils were the highest barrier to raising standards', blaming the students themselves rather than the increasingly behaviourist and repressive school framework recommended by government. From this assertion can be followed the anti-student strategy of the NASUWT, as they increasingly targeted so-called 'disruptive' students and their families.

From 1993-95 there were many stories in the press about school exclusions, often prompted by surveys or reports from OFSTED. In December 1993, inspectors reported on a worrying increase in the numbers of primary school pupils being excluded for bad behaviour. 'Bad teachers', they argued were a part of the problem, in particular those who showed 'a lack of preparation or organisation'.[4] Their report was dismissed by the NASUWT as 'a waste of space' that was 'too pious for its own good'. At the conference of the British Psychological Society in April 1995, educational psychologist and researcher, André Imich claimed that school students were being excluded more and more to 'impress parents' and 'boost schools' reputations for strict discipline',[5] while at the conference of the Metropolitan Authorities in the previous January, it was reported that more and more pupils from the age of five were out of the control of teachers and were being excluded from school.[6]

It should be noted that many of these exclusions were being provoked by the new requirements for league tables, truancy rates and unauthorised absences that had been introduced in February 1993 by John Patten, then the Secretary of State for Education. By permanently excluding students, a school's figures could miraculously improve – expelling chronic truants became a way of 'tidying up' the truancy figures.[7] By September 1995, the number of exclusions was becoming so embarrassing for the government that the *Times Educational Supplement* reported that ministers were involved in seeking to cover them up, after a government-sponsored report by Carl Parsons of Christchurch College in Canterbury showed that the number of 'permanent exclusions' in more than a hundred LEAs across the country had reached 10,000.[8] Thus the market system which was developing in schools fed into the growing culture of repression: it fuelled the increase in expulsions which then had to be justified by resort to righteous indignation about declining standards of behaviour. For example, Headteachers represented by the National Association of Headteachers were now demanding stronger expulsion powers as, they claimed, children were becoming 'violent at an earlier age'.[9]

THE IMPACT OF JAMES BULGER'S MURDER

When two eleven-year-old Merseyside boys were convicted of the abduction from a shopping mall and murder of two-year-old James Bulger in November 1993, the tabloid press seemed to seize the pretext to label an entire generation of children as 'evil'. The 'child' became the 'enemy'. The *Daily Mail*[10] carried a sixteen-page supplement on the case, while the *Daily Express*[11] had an eight-page one. *The Times'*[12] editorial of 25 November declared that 'childhood has a darker side which past societies perhaps understood better than our own' and described three species of 'evil': 'metaphysical evil – the imperfection of all mankind; physical evil – the suffering that human beings cause each other; and moral evil – the choice of vice over virtue. Children are separated by necessity of age from none of these'. The two convicted 11-year-olds were demonised as 'monsters' or 'animals', or, as headlined on the front page of the *Daily Mirror*[13] under their school photographs, 'freaks of nature with hearts of unparalleled evil'. They were branded as 'the children from hell'. On the day following the convictions, the *Mirror's*[14] editorial pledged the paper's commitment to 'wage war on the army of truants' – among whom were James Bulger's 'little killers'. To effect this, there must also be 'an army of truant officers. It is not just a matter of hand wringing and head shaking over the figures'. As the front page headline proclaimed: 'Patrols to hunt truant terrors'.[15]

Suddenly, the demonisation that had been largely reserved for black children was being accorded to all working class children, black and white. They were all 'evil', part of a dark 'army of children hanging around streets and shopping centres', as *The Times Educational Supplement*[16] put it, also on their front page. Quoting spokespersons from the nation's second-largest police force, the West Midlands Constabulary, the article revealed that 'in two days last month the force found that more than a quarter of the 'truants' stopped in the city centre were children who have been suspended or expelled'. These were the denizens of the new territories of the damned, like James Bulger's killers. 'We were concerned at the high number of excluded children,' said Sergeant Jean White, the force's public liaison officer: 'Some can be out of school for up to two years and something needs to be done to occupy their time constructively'. The 'children who roam the malls' were becoming the new menace, and teachers, police, social workers and public were being given their firm commission to retrieve their lives. These reactions to the death of James Bulger seemed to signal the final abandonment of approaching children as rational, meaning-making, thinking people. Instead we all had to be on our guards against them, with teachers becoming the prime sentinels. Any vestiges of child-centredness, or echoes of the theme of the Plowden Report of the late 1960s – 'At the heart of the educational process is the child' – must now be set aside: the illusion of child-trustfulness could no longer have a place in the institutional mind of the school.

THE ADVENTURES OF RICHARD

On 23 April 1996, the students and teachers of Glaisdale School in Bilborough, a working-class area of Nottingham, awoke to find their school all over the front and inside pages of national newspapers. The cause was the exclusion of one student, 13-year-old Richard Wilding, his subsequent winning of an appeal and return to the school, and the refusal of its NASUWT members to teach him – they threatened to strike if he returned to mainstream classes. In the wake of the death of James Bulger, Richard – who according to the *Daily Mail*[17] 'played truant and was often seen in the shopping parade' near his home – was soon, as he himself described it so accurately, 'tarred by all of this'. The *Daily Mirror*[18] portrayed him as a 'yob – a schoolboy thug'; the *Sun*[19] described him as a 'boy lout, a yob of the form', who had brought his entire school 'to the brink of closure'. *The Guardian* [20] questioned whether he was not 'the worst pupil in Britain' under a full-page portrait of him in its Tuesday education supplement – while quoting a local education offi-cer as saying 'we're stuck with him'. The *Mail* labelled him as 'the boy who spells trouble', telling its readers of a grim family pathology: 'If you think this one's unruly, you should see his brother'. Bernard Dineen, a columnist on the *Yorkshire Post*, [21] recommended that Richard's mother be sent on a compulsory 'civic education' course to learn 'how to become a mother'. For the *Daily Telegraph* the affair was an opportunity to urge a swift return to corporal punishment in schools.[22] It was clear that the language used to describe Richard was drawing on the imagery evoked by the Bulger case.

Richard's parents had used their legal right to appeal against their son's exclusion, seeking to safeguard his entitle-ment to mainstream secondary education. They did so correctly and successfully, and not without some effort, as his father, a former industrial cleaner, suffered from severe ill-health. When he collapsed and died, a week after the mass of public exposure that surrounded his son's case, the *Daily Mail* headlined its report 'Yob's father dies'. Richard had no doubt given his teachers some problems, and offered them complex challenges. But this did not justify the barrage of press abuse directed at him and his family. There were very few who took Richard's side: in the national newspapers there was an article in the *Independent*,[23] by this author, two weeks after the events, and there was one other in the

Morning Star, together with some letters in *The Times Educational Supplement*. As one letter made clear, Richard and his family were the last in the pecking order; and their 'pecking back', to the extent of carrying through and winning their legal appeal, could not be tolerated: 'Richard Wilding is not the "child from hell" nor does he represent the "modern malaise". He is only a 13-year-old boy. The Government blames the teachers, then teachers blame parents. Now it seems that badly behaved little boys are behind the problem'.[24]

Another right-wing teachers' association featured tales of infant terrrorism at its conference in April 1996, when members of the Association of Teachers and Lecturers (ATL), meeting in Torquay, raised the case of a nine-year-old boy behaving so violently that his teacher was permanently injured. Instead of hearing the full story, those present were told of the incident only in relation to the serious consequences for the teacher. How could the child be treated so that such an incident could never happen again in the classroom? How does a teacher counsel a child who is so distressed? How can his community become directly involved in supporting both the student and the school? None of these questions was considered. To learn more of the case required the efforts of investigative journalism and an explanatory article in the *Independent*;[25] those sufficiently interested then discovered that the child was a recent refugee from Zaire who had personally witnessed the atrocities and violent conflict in his homeland in 1992. The draconian impulses of some teachers' unions were expressed again at the 1996 non-TUC affiliated Professional Association of Teachers conference at Cheltenham. Its members called for the withdrawal of child benefit from parents who miss parents' evenings or fail to ensure that their children are in school.

DISCIPLINE OR OPPORTUNISM?

Other similar cases were coming to light, where headlines were focused on the trials of teachers in dealing with troublesome children, with no information at all – or sympathy – being given to the circumstances of the children themselves. The boisterousness of some of these liable-to-be-excluded children, and their inclination to become excitable or disruptive, were often caused by their medical condition. Yet they were being treated in the same dismissive, exclusory way. Six-year-old Andrew Eaton was excluded from his school in Trafford, Manchester, after his parents had refused to sign a 'home-school' contract, promising he would behave in a disciplined manner. Andrew had allegedly bullied other pupils, thrown equipment around and bitten a teacher. It later emerged that he had been diagnosed by a doctor as having the medical condition Attention Deficit Hyperactivity Disorder.[26]

Also in Nottingham, this time it was a group of parents who sought the removal of an eight-year-old black pupil from Seeley Church of England School. Kyle Bent had been disruptive in lessons, and psychologists had diagnosed that his behaviour too was caused by ADHD. The teachers knew this and mostly thought that Kyle should remain in the school while receiving proper medical attention and the extra resources that would enable him to have more teacher attention. In this case, the negative actions of the unsympathetic parents were resisted and, although some protested by withdrawing their children from the school, teachers and governors stood firm and backed the child and inclusive educational principles.[27]

Meanwhile, at Hebburn Comprehensive School in South Tyneside, the NASUWT were again refusing to teach a pupil, Graham Cram, whom they had profiled as 'violent'. In this case police were called to warn the boy's father to leave the school premises after he had accompanied his son there to ensure that he was not taught in isolation from other students. He had exercised his right to appeal after Graham's 'permanent exclusion' and had been successful. The NASUWT had blocked the boy's return and their action prevailed when the LEA agreed that they would be allowed to continue to refuse to teach him.[28] The union's General Secretary claimed that the union had 'struck a blow for the maintenance of good order', [29] and that its objective was to abolish appeals panels – the only democratic recourse for excluded children to return to the school from which they have been excluded. In a letter to *The Times*, he described the appeals panels as nothing more than mechanisms for 'irresponsible parents demanding the right to send their children to mainstream schools regardless of their offspring's behaviour'.[30]

As these incidents came and went, rarely ending with any solution that would benefit the excluded students or the pursuit of inclusive education, a report was published which put the entire issue of the exclusion of working-class and black students in its true context. In *Poverty: The Facts*,[31] the Child Poverty Action Group revealed that one in every three children in Britain was growing up in poverty. In 1979, the ratio had been one in ten. By 1996, 4.3 million British children were living within this category. And yet families in poor circumstances – like many of those whose children were being excluded from school – were being blamed for the very ills against which their families were struggling. 'Poverty results from misguided social and economic policy rather than personal failure', commented Sally Witcher, the CPAG's spokesperson, and she called on politicians to act upon facts rather than on prejudice and opportunism.[32]

During the same week, Shadow Education Secretary David Blunkett was following a familiar routine of spin and high profile press coverage. In banner headlines on the front page of the *Daily Express* was the message 'Red Card for unruly pupils: Labour's plan to blow whistle on classroom violence'.[33] In the following article were Blunkett's new proposals on school discipline to be made to the forthcoming conference of the Association of Teachers and Lecturers: 'Football-style red and yellow cards will be introduced to curb classroom hooligans if Labour wins the next election'. This 'exclusive' in the *Daily Express* was hugely effective. The football imagery endorsed procedures of control that are used to manage an activity of mechanical rule processes, where one person, the referee, has total authority; this was to become the proposed framework for organising that most complex and heterogeneous of human organisations – an inner-city school. Such a strategy had behind it the support and communicative means of one of the nation's foremost Tory newspapers, with a mass readership. The editorial on the facing page revealed why: 'What does 'new' Labour think it is – the Tory party?'

Although instituted by the Conservatives, this lethal educational mix of market policies backed up by authoritarian control systems has been retained and extended by New Labour. One example of this is the revival of the notion of the 'sin bin' or internal exclusion unit. The *Daily Mail*, in its 'Education Notebook' of 10 November 1998, observed that Education Secretary David Blunkett was backing the setting up of in-school support units or sin bins, as they are more commonly known. The *Mail* article goes on to describe a unit in one Derbyshire school 'which looks like a bright, inviting classroom', while continually referring to it as a 'sin bin'. Thus the committed work of teachers to tackle exclusion in the school (which had dropped by 40 per cent), and to bring back the students' motivation to learn, was undermined. The organiser of the unit was quoted as arguing that the success of the project 'lies in the fact that there is no stigma on the child'. The *Mail*'s report, in contrast, reinforces the old stigmatisation.

A CLASS ISSUE

In August 1998, the broadsheets were reporting extensively on the stark divisions between success and failure in the British education system, in their coverage of the yearly GCSE results. A *Guardian* leader lamented the 'widening of the gap between the top and the bottom',[34] quoting at length the general secretary of the National Association of Head Teachers, who asserted that the competitive nature of school league tables was 'creating an educational underclass' of excluded youth and pressurising schools to concentrate upon students who were likely to bring the school strong examination success. 'There is no doubt whatsoever that performance tables, in their current form, are damaging the educational health of low achievers,' he declared. *The Times* education correspondent observed that the emergence of this 'education underclass' posed 'a new challenge to the government's Social Exclusion Unit'.[35] It was clear that New Labour's continuation of Conservative policies and demagoguery was creating more of the same rejection, failure and exclusion. Yet there was still no serious attempt to address issues of exclusion, or to try to understand the sources of excluded children's difficulties.

Thus David Blunkett's 1998 speech to the Labour Party Conference set out an authoritarian strategy for dealing with truants and excluded school students. He recommended police snatch squads and sophisticated computerised surveillance technology for the truants and 'special units' and 'sin bins' for the excluded students.[36] There was no mention of any possible causes of disaffection, in the curriculum or the ethos of schools. He also announced plans to split teachers through 'payment by performance' and the creation of a few highly paid Advanced Skills teachers or 'superteacher' posts. Blunkett is absolutely resolute in his search for educational solutions that ignore structural problems; instead he relies on disciplining (mainly) or rewarding (divisively) individual teachers or pupils. Yet, as once more evidenced in a *Times Educational Supplement*[37] report on a survey involving 5000 school students in the London borough of Ealing, it is structural problems that cause problems in schools. The study revealed, again, that it is social class that forms the determining factor in a child's performance at school. 'Poor social conditions must be tackled before there will be a rise in pupil performance', the report concluded. Here was yet more evidence that exclusion from success in education is primarily an issue of class, and that no authoritarianism or divide-and-rule tactics would change that. But new Labour have made no strategic attempt to create an inclusive school system, and to develop policies which prioritise need – instead they focus on image, 'orders' and tabloid rhetoric.

Sure enough, in October 1998, the Home Office, quoting Section 16 of the Crime and Disorder Act, announced new powers allowing the police to pick up truants and escort them back to school, together with 'truancy watch' and 'pupil pass' schemes.[38] According to *The Times Educational Supplement*, the 'crackdown' is part of what the Government calls its 'joined-up thinking', with education policy linking with Home Office policy to reduce youth crime. A 'Government source' was quoted: 'No longer will getting excluded be seen as a soft option'.[39] As if it ever were to large numbers of black and working-class youth, who now in addition to 'stop and search' faced new forms of arrest, harassment and denial of their rights. And by March 2001, Blunkett had extended his authoritarian remedies to the parents of 'disruptive' school students, who were to be given compulsory 'special parenting classes' to deal with their 'deficiencies'.[40]

REFERENCES

1. Jenny Bourne, Lee Bridges and Chris Searle, *Outcast England*, Institute of Race Relations, London 1994.
2. *Daily Mail*, 28.8.96.
3. *The Times*, 25.10.94.
4. *Guardian*, 14.12.93.
5. *Guardian*, 4.4.95.
6. *Guardian*, 31.1.95.
7. *Daily Telegraph*, 20.2.93.
8. *Times Educational Supplement*, 14.7.95.
9. *Guardian*, 22.9.95.
10. *Daily Mail*, 25.11.93.
11. *Daily Express*, 25.11.93.
12. *The Times*, 25.11.93.
13. *Daily Mirror*, 25.11.93.
14. *Daily Mirror*, 26.11.93.
15. For an excellent account of the newspaper reporting of the James Bulger murder trial, see Bob Franklin and Julian Petley: 'Killing the Age of Innocents: Newspaper Reporting of the Death of James Bulger in Jane Pilcher and Stephen Wagg (eds), *Thatcher's Children*, Falmer Press, London 1996.
16. *Times Educational Supplement*, 19.11.93.
17. *Daily Mail*, 23.4.96.
18. *Daily Mirror*, 23.4.96.

19. *The Sun*, 23.4.96.
20. *The Guardian*, 23.4.96.
21. *Yorkshire Post*, 30.4.96.
22. *Daily Telegraph*, 23.4.96.
23. *Independent*, 29.4.96.
24. *Times Educational Supplement*, 3.5.96.
25. *Independent*, 29.4.96.
26. *Times Educational Supplement*, 3.5.96.
27. *Guardian*, 4.6.96.
28. *Guardian*, 14.5.96.
29. *Morning Star*, 14.5.96.
30. *The Times*, 24.5.96.
31. Carey Oppenhein and Lisa Harker, *Poverty: The Facts*, Child Poverty Action Group, London 1996.
32. *Morning Star*, 18.4.96.
33. *Daily Express*, 2.4.96.
34. *Guardian*, 27.8.98.
35. *The Times*, 27.8.98.
36. *Times Educational Supplement*, 1.10.98.
37. *Times Educational Supplement*, 25.9.98.
38. *'New police powers to stop truanting begin tomorrow'*, Home Office News Release 470/98, 30.11.98.
39. *Times Educational Supplement*, 2.10.98.
40. *Guardian*, 25.3.01.

CHAPTER 5

Exclusion and Moralism

The end of the twentieth century brought with it an assault of huge and pervasive power on the people of our inner cities; two decades of Conservative economic neoliberalism and social authoritarianism left many feeling impoverished and powerless. A burden of depredation and suffering was laid upon Britain's poorest people, and has grown heavier every year. Yet New Labour, the inheritors of these backward decades, are fashioning a new political force that aims to increase the marketisation of society, and continues to deploy much of the existing superstructure of legislation, from the anti-Trade Union Laws to the Criminal Justice, Sentencing and Education Acts. New Labour demonstrates a will to create not a politics of class and community, going back to roots, but a politics of assumed virtue and rhetoric of moralism. As so often, moralism is the companion of authoritarianism. Moral deficiency is seen as the source of problems rather than underlying structural causes.

Whereas 'Old Labour' saw the violence of poverty as its enemy and the working class as the foundation of reform, 'New Labour' blames its victims for their poverty and sees upward mobility and middle-class moralism as its bedrock. Thus the most vulnerable in British life in the meltdown of the welfare state – the homeless, the beggars, the never-employed, the 'squeegee merchants', the single mothers, the asylum-seekers and refugees, the excluded school students, the frustrated children on decaying council estates – are neglected, marginalised and criminalised. During the General Election campaign of 1997, huge posters proclaiming that 'Young offenders will be punished' were put up on billboards by New Labour in council estates and working-class neighbourhoods all over Britain, as threats were transformed into slogans and advertisements.

Morality, what is right and what is wrong, is being debased to moralism, making judgements about other people's morality. Thus where one party (the Tories) threatens the revival of the cane and proposes a military cadet force in every school, its 'opposition' (New Labour) commends a nightly curfew for working-class youth in inner-city neighbourhoods. New Labour papers over the sheer gulfs of class, replacing a socialist ideology with the same icons and moralism which characterise the forces they claim to oppose – and all under the guise of the 'moral crusade'. By and large, New Labour continues the old-school moral authoritarianism of Thatcher and Major; but this trend is reinforced by its terror of being seen as Old Labour or in any sense 'soft' (and this is a measure of the political defeats of the 1980s and 1990s, from which Labour has yet to recover). Furthermore, New Labour's increasing managerialism means that the language of emancipation, which used to be part of the Labour Party's approach to education, has been replaced by an obsession with inputs, outputs and efficiency, the educational parlance of targets, standards and outcomes. In managerial terms, disruptive students impair the smooth functioning of the system.

DR TATE'S MEDICINE

In 1996, the government's chief curriculum advisor, Dr Nicholas Tate, chief executive of the Qualifications and Curriculum Authority (QCA), announced that 'a moral watchdog' was to be established to 'lay down standards for every school in Britain'.[1] The next day, a *Guardian* leader remembered the insights of philosopher Bertrand Russell: 'Bertrand Russell was right. Britain has always enjoyed two kinds of morality side by side: one we preach but do not practise, and another which we practise but seldom preach'.[2]

These two paradigms serve as a distinction between moralism and morality. The Steve Bell cartoon adjacent to the editorial expressed them in graphic form. On a blackboard draped with a Union flag, beside a pulpit and before a line of school desks, a parody of the 'Lord's Prayer' has been chalked:

Our Churchill which art in Nelson
Hallowed be thy Rhodes. Thy Gradgrind come.
Thy Smiles be done in Kent as it is in Surrey.
Give us this day our *Daily Mail*
And forgive us our Socialists, as we
Forgive them that organise against us (NOT!)
And lead us not into trade unionism,
But deliver us from Scargill
For thine is the Jingo
The Land of Hope and Glory.
For ever and ever
School without roof
Amen

Tate's announcement came at a conference bringing together the top echelons of 'educationalists and church leaders'.[3] A message from Sir Ron Dearing, who had come to the government's aid in paring down the initially unworkable National Curriculum, backed the crusade, calling for a 'sense of rage' against 'escalating violence and the breakdown of civilised values'.[4] It was the beginning of a 'moral mission', declared Sir Ron, with the curriculum objective being nothing less than to 'renew civilisation'. Schools, said Tate, should each formulate a 'mission statement', which 'spelled out clear views about what was right and what children should be taught'. He endorsed his own advocacy of a 'majority culture which was sure of itself', and which would define the ethos and state-licensed cultural hegemony of the National Curriculum.[5]

In a leading article in the *Daily Express*, Tate warned that without recourse to such reinforcement of explicit codes of public morality in schools, 'social cohesion is potentially under threat': the nation's young people would 'go round thinking that there is no difference between morality and taste'.[6] Far from tracing the causes of this moral crisis in the market system and the notions expressed by Margaret Thatcher's 'there is no such thing as society', Tate blamed the state of affairs on the 'climate of political correctness'. 'Recognition that there are differences between cultures and groups', he declared, 'has led to the view that there are no longer values relevant to everyone. It has weakened the very concept of a set of core beliefs'.

In a later article in *The Times*, under the pious headline 'Deliver us from these fallacies', Tate reminded his readers that building the moral crusade: 'means reviving our sense that we belong to a civic society with a shared moral code and a common culture. It means that there is a moral dimension to every aspect of our lives'.[7] In the same issue his photograph appeared under the banner of the 'National Forum for

Values in Education and the Community', introducing a draft moral code for schools, and declaring that: 'We value truth, human rights, the law, justice and collective endeavour for the common good of society'. Directly below was another story, reporting that the government was giving schools more power to select the students of their choice, and pledging to move forward and realise Prime Minister Major's dream of a 'grammar school in every town'. Tate responded with an assertion that moral education 'could lead to improved examination results', citing schools in some of the Pacific Rim nations like South Korea and Singapore as examples, despite their poor records of democracy.[8]

THE 'ME-FIRST' ETHOS

The 'moral crusade' initiative created much public froth and excitement in the establishment press, provoking invocations to corporal punishment, hanging, curfews and boot camps. Against all this moral indignation, a letter in *The Times*, from a John Drake of Billericay, stood out.[9] He asked of John Major: 'Does this mean he will now reject the policies which the Tory Government have pursued for the past 17 years, and its "me-first" ethos, which have done so much to damage our society and to create the conditions in which social irresponsibility, lawlessness and violence breed?'

By November 1996, the government's own figures showed that almost a third of British babies were being born into poverty – so much for morality. 'The face of poverty is increasingly a child's face', observed shadow Social Security Minister Malcolm Hicks.[10] A report based on government information on the number of people in Britain claiming income support published in December 1996, showed that there were more than 5.8 million – an 18.2 per cent increase since the General Election of 1992.[11] Other data demonstrated that people in such conditions of poverty were much more likely to suffer ill health. A report from the Department of Health made this disparity of class clear:

Life expectancy at birth was seven years higher in social class one (professional) than in social class five (manual). Children in social class five were four times more likely to suffer accidental death than their peers in social class one. Of 66 major causes of death in men, 62 were more common in the social classes four and five combined than in other social classes. Of 70 major causes of death in women, 64 were more common to women married to men in social classes four and five.[12]

So much for Major's promises of a 'classless society' and the foundation stones of a moral crusade – this was the working out in reality of Tate's tendentious suggestion that 'the market will answer even moral questions'.[13] In the midst of the 1997 General Election campaign *The Guardian* (28.4.97) revealed that the European Union statistics agency had published a report showing that Britain had more children living in poverty (one in three), than any other European country; moreover, the Government had expended strenuous efforts to conceal these facts.

For those living on the extreme margins of British society, this recourse to public morality was grimly ironic. As the Government brought in its Asylum Bill, at least 30,000 refugees and asylum seekers were being threatened with the loss of their housing benefit, income support and their children's free school meals; living with the spectre of impending deportation, they were now facing destitution and homelessness, as their remaining cash benefits came to be replaced by supermarket vouchers. This was the other side of the core set of national beliefs. Under this new legislation asylum seekers have been forcibly dispersed to vacant, sub-standard housing all over the country, consigned to estates where no-one else wants to live, liable to arbitrary arrest by immigration officers.

The debate over the Asylum bill legitimated the return to public discourse of a racist and exclusivist account of nationhood. This helped to create a violent and xenophobic atmosphere. Violence against black people increased, as did arrests and police interference in the lives of refugees and other people regarded as outsiders. Violent racists targeted refugees and single black mothers in London's most dangerous neighbourhoods.[14] Brian Douglas, an African-Caribbean who died after being arrested in Clapham, south London in May 1995, was the first person in Britain to die as a result of the Metropolitan Police's use of newly-introduced American-style solid acrylic batons[15] (these were twice the weight of the defunct truncheons that had killed London teacher Blair Peach in 1979). In December 1995 Wayne Douglas, another black man, died in Brixton Police Station, after also being struck by the new weapon. Ibrahim Sey, a Ghanaian born asylum-seeker, died in March 1996 after being arrested outside his East London home. He had volunteered for peaceful arrest, and was taken to Ilford Police Station, where he was assaulted, handcuffed and sprayed by the police's new CS gas.[16] Vijay Singh, a thirteen-year-old boy from Stretford, Manchester hanged himself from the banisters of his home after being continually taunted at school and called 'bobble head' because of his Sikh gota.[17] In Glasgow, Labour MP George Galloway accused the British immigration authorities of 'bearing a major responsibility' for the avoidable death of Mohammed Yaqoob, a relative of a local Pakistani family who came to Britain for a heart by-pass operation: immigration officials blocked his entry lest he overstayed his visa deadline, even though his family had raised funds for his treatment at a Glasgow private hospital.[18] Such were the realities behind the rhetoric of the 'National Forum for Values in Education and the Community', and its claims to 'human rights, the law, justice and collective endeavour' that Tate was simultaneously proclaiming.

STAMPEDE TO MORALISM

Tate identified three crucial factors that led him to call for a 'moral crusade'.[19] One was the massacre of primary school children in Dunblane, in Scotland, by a man who had been given open access to handguns. Another was the Prince of Wales' call for a 'genuine celebration of the millennium'. The third was the public revulsion at the stabbing to death in 1995 of London headteacher Philip Lawrence, as he went to help a student who was being attacked by another youth outside the school. His wife Frances Lawrence was featured on the front pages of almost every national newspaper calling for a 'moral manifesto for the nation' as a memorial to her husband's ideas.[20] She declared that society must begin to address the issue 'of despised and rejected' young people and advocated a ban on selling weapon-type knives. She proposed that 'citizenship' should be stressed in the curricula of schools, that teachers and the police should be afforded higher status and that the values of family life should be emphasised. She hoped to see a nationwide movement to banish violence and encourage 'civic values'. Establishment politicians, those who ruled and their New Labour shadows, plunged in to grasp the moral opportunity. The *Guardian* observed:

> Conservatives, Labour and Liberal Democrats began a stampede yesterday to claim they were the closest to the moral agenda for the regeneration of Britain set out by the widow of Philip Lawrence, the murdered headteacher.

On a day which saw politics, morality and religion mixing unhappily together, the parties vied with one another to lead Frances Lawrence's national movement to renew civic values amongst Britain's young.[21]

A year after his death, during the unveiling of a plaque of remembrance to the headteacher outside the gates of St George's Roman Catholic School in north west London, the politicians were in attendance alongside the hierarchy of the Catholic Church. Labour Shadow Home Secretary Jack Straw, who had not long before suggested curfews for teenagers and made condemnatory remarks against London's homeless and 'squeegee merchants' was there, as was Home Secretary Michael Howard, the architect of anti-asylum seeker and anti-refugee legislation, and currently engaged in arming the police and installing new repressive measures against inner city and black youth. Howard spoke at the service of 'turning away from the barrenness of despair', reminding the assembly of Mrs Lawrence's 'message of hope and redemption', and proclaiming that 'love and reason would triumph over hate and irrationality'.[22]

It is particularly unedifying when populist politicians attempt to corral personal tragedy into service in the ideological battle over morality, and such recourse is always fraught with contradiction. Yet Philip Lawrence himself, though his courage cannot be gainsaid, embodied some of the contradictions in a moralist agenda for schools. In a radio interview given shortly before his death and published in the *Daily Telegraph* following his murder, he identified one major strategy for changing his school and dealing with internal disruption.[23] This was the permanent exclusion of the students deemed to be demotivated and troublesome. Some sixty students had been expelled during his two-year headship at the school. It was a terrible irony that the youth convicted of his murder was also an excluded student, but from a neighbouring school.[24] Exclusions are known to feed the growth of criminal gangs in many inner city areas, and cleansing classrooms of reluctant or rebellious school students only exposes them to the dangerous environment of the streets, where they vent their frustration and play to new rules to win peer approval.

Mrs Lawrence's compassionate attitude towards the youth convicted of her husband's murder ('My heart goes out to him and his family. I felt a great sadness for him ...)[25] was undermined by the racist and scurrilous article published adjacent to her words in the *Daily Mirror*. Opposite a dignified family photograph of Lawrence and his children relaxing in their London garden before his death is the photo and profile of the foreign and black Learco Chindamo, 'the evil little scumbag who killed Philip Lawrence'. The two families are placed next to each other as antitheses. Lawrence's widow is professional, articulate and white. Chindamo's mother is Filipino, unemployed and an immigrant: 'As far as I can work out', read the column, 'the only connection between his family and Britain is that his mother wanted a deep and meaningful relationship with our welfare state'. And it goes on to condemn a Labour council (Camden) for 'handing out accommodation to any immigrant who wanted it'. Coming back to Chindamo's mother, the article labels her a 'stupid cow', and exclaims that 'the best of Britain is being murdered by the very worst'. The step from a moralism based on such 'British' values to a virulent racism is a short one.

MANTON AND THE RIDINGS

When the case of the murder of Philip Lawrence came to court, as with the murdered infant James Bulger, a new campaign to demonise young people was set loose in the tabloid press.[26] In a typical article, the 'News Focus' double-page spread in the *Sunday Mirror* headlined the 'evil behind the innocence' of youths involved in gang warfare, and condemned 'the violent reign of terror in our class-rooms', beside a photograph of Philip Lawrence.[27] There was also the case of Matthew Wilson, labelled the 'nation's most notorious schoolboy' in *The Times Educational Supplement,* see pp8–9).[28] Intimate details of Matthew's school disciplinary record became public knowledge across the land and confidentiality became an irrelevance. A similar national humiliation was suffered by thirteen-year-old Sarah Taylor when she became the centre of NASUWT action in The Ridings School, Halifax. The *Daily Mail* carried the headline 'Morality in crisis' because she had given birth to a baby girl. The story began, 'A mother at 13, far from the innocent face of Ridings', and it ended with the intrusive and condemning words of a local Conservative councillor: 'How is that mother going to be able to pass on to her daughter the responsibility of life?'[29] The *Daily Express* headline read 'a baby for the mother of all school tearaways'.[30]

These two students and their parents had committed the cardinal sin of exercising their democratic right of appeal against permanent exclusion, successfully gaining reinstate-ment in their respective schools. Such appeals should be abolished, repeated the General Secretary of the NASUWT. In a letter to *The Times* de Gruchy he described them as forums for 'irresponsible parents demanding the right to send their children to mainstream schools regardless of their offspring's behaviour.' [31]

And yet much of the education system had descended into a crisis of exclusion. Permanent exclusions had increased by two-thirds in the previous three years, with only 15 per cent of those excluded from secondary schools returning to any other school.[32] Local Education Authorities were becoming more and more disinclined to provide funding for high-cost alternative provision for excluded students, and a Department of Education and Employment (DfEE) official was quoted as saying that there would be fewer and fewer 'goodies for baddies'. Professor Carl Parsons of Christchurch College, Canterbury, organiser of a national survey of exclusions, revealed large scale increases in students being excluded from primary as well as secondary schools (including 4-year-olds).[33] Nationally there were 13,400 official exclusions – and an estimated of thousands more 'unofficial' expulsions – with many of the excluded students finding only a few hours desultory tuition a week at a 'pupil referral unit'. This, observed Parsons, was 'a source of professional and political shame'.[34]

The moral panic about exclusions involved an uneasy oscillation between concern for and fear of excluded students. The *Guardian* warned in an editorial of 'the emergence of a fifth column of disaffected and excluded pupils with a high potential for crime';[35] and from the upper tiers of the Anglican church, Archbishop of Canterbury George Carey gave an austere prophecy of alienated young British males 'biting back in a spectacular fashion' against the system that was excluding them. He warned that: 'If we fail to address with real urgency, and in a spirit of human solidarity, the vast problems being stored up in the form of angry, disappointed young people who feel that mainstream society has no time or place for them, we shall reap a hitter harvest'.[36] With neo-Swiftian satire, Colin Crouch of Bognor Regis, in the *Education Guardian* letters page, compared the situation of expelled schoolchildren with that of cattle suffering from the BSE epidemic. He offered his own 'modest proposal':

> We have an exactly similar situation with BSE in cattle, where again the situation was created by collusion between the government and society. It was no use hoping that good advice to farmers would make it go away: there had to be a huge and terrible cull.
>
> Isn't it time to look clearly and honestly at the schooling system we have created and however terrible this may seem, apply to it the same healing, cauterising remedy?
>
> Of course, there will be pain. Of course, there will be outcry. But I believe in five years we will have solved the problem of expulsions, and removed forever from our schools the threat of indiscipline and delinquency. Then truly, there will be grammar schools for all.[37]

The NASUWT continued to view the situation from the other end, blaming students even though they were frequently the most vulnerable victims of the economic and social circumstances in which the school found itself. The cost of educating 'disruptive' and statemented children in mainstream schools was the major cause of government cutbacks in education, it claimed. The victims were those who must be blamed: 'integrating emotionally disturbed children into mainstream education, who would previously have gone to special schools, has been a policy disaster on a par with care in the community'.[38] Since a grossly disproportionate number of excluded students were from black communities, black parents (and grandparents) found themselves projected a quarter of a century back into history, fighting again against the dumping of their children into sin-bins or schools for the 'educationally sub-normal'.

As passions grew about a serious student behaviour situation in The Ridings School in Halifax, where the NASUWT were calling for mass exclusions, de Gruchy publicly proclaimed the stance of Philip Lawrence on exclusions, praising the sixty exclusions Lawrence had made during his 'all too brief period as headteacher at St George's School'.[39] This was the very proportion (approximately one in ten of the student population of the school) that his members at The Ridings wished to exclude. He made his loyalty clear: 'Pupils don't pay subscriptions, members do'.[40] Although he considered the 'morality' campaign 'bloody crap' (according to *The Times Educational Supplement*), he asserted that his members were seeking the betterment of school life by stemming the tide of violence and disruption.[41]

Meanwhile, the continuing saga over Matthew Wilson at Manton School (see pp8–9) bled on, with new human targets and victims. Parents were divided against parents, and a long-serving and dedicated chair of governors who had defended the stigmatised Matthew Wilson was humiliated and forced to resign: 'I have been made out to be a witch on a broom-stick,' she said.[42] Matthew's mother, facing up to the merciless press hounding and public abuse of her son (he had been compelled at one point to hide under a car from hostile tabloid journalists and cameramen) was quoted in despair: 'I can't win, no matter what I do. If I take him to another school then all the parents there will say they don't want him either.'[43]

BEHIND THE MORAL FACADE

Exclusions and their consequences were only one manifestation of the prevailing immoral educational processes and structures – structures that attacked working-class and black families, creating injustice, inequality, frustration and desperation among parents and young people. Even the traditionally conservative *Times Educational Supplement* asserted in its editorial that the crisis at The Ridings, blamed by the NASUWT leadership and tabloid journalists on 'unteachable' students and bad parenting, in fact ' … looks like the market mechanism at work' and 'government policies coming home to roost'.[44] Its leader article noted that a high proportion of the pupils on the NASUWT's alleged hit-list for exclusion had already been excluded or otherwise rejected from local grant-maintained schools, and were thus finding their true place within the market system, among the wastage and unsaleable goods. For The Ridings school itself was an amalgam of two working class secondary modern schools serving council estates, established to give a 'comprehensive' schooling to children unable to obtain places in the two selective grant-maintained grammar schools that had 'opted out' of LEA control and taken extra funding from central government. As local MP Alice Mahon made clear, these privileged government-funded schools stood in stark contrast to the hard-pressed Ridings, with its 20 students who had been expelled from neighbouring schools and 135 others struggling with special educational needs.[45] Added to this, the local Calderdale LEA had lost £18 million from its education budget in six years, because of the 'opting out' of the grammar schools. The 'two-tier' system became inevitable, and illustrated precisely what provoked selection.

But though the crisis at The Ridings had largely resulted from the increasing role of the market in the education system, ever-increasing selection in education remained among the most pressing priorities for the Major government. As the Ridings crisis escalated – once more clearly illustrating the intimate link between free enterprise and authoritarianism – the Government introduced a further education bill to give schools more power to select and reject students, and to allocate more funds to the 'assisted places' scheme by which selected families received grants for private education. Selective largesse was now to be extended to exclusive 'prep' schools in the private junior sector.[46] Meanwhile, the reality of the bipartisan new moralism was manifest in the decisions by both leader Tony Blair and shadow minister, Harriet Harman to send their own children to selective grant-maintained schools some considerable distance from their homes.

In other 'moral' steps forward, the then Secretary of State for Education Gillian Shepherd proposed that infant teachers be obliged to test all 5-year-olds within six months of their entry into school,[47] and a few weeks later she was championing the cause of corporal punishment in schools as a 'useful deterrent to bad behaviour', with the full support of the tabloid press. The *Sun* saw a 'glimmer of hope ... of bringing back the cane'.[48] This was, however, negated by the Prime Minister.

Unfortunately for those who make no connection between morality and the market system, the hidden hand of the market will not deliver a morally justifiable school system. In fact the market always pushes the system towards injustice. It is inevitable that competition between schools will reinforce a division between failing and successful schools. Thus it is crucial that schools do well in school league tables: otherwise they will be set on a downward spiral of falling rolls and diminishing resources. This has led to yet another form of selection. It was revealed in August 1996 that, in an effort to boost their performance in the tables, schools were refusing thousands of sixteen-year-olds their right to sit GCSE examinations. As they strove to beat their rivals in the number of GCSE passes obtained, in particular trying to score well on the percentage of those achieving five GCSE passes between grades A and C, candidates deemed 'doubtful' passers were not allowed to attempt the exam, on the grounds that their results would bring down the school's overall pass rate, and that all efforts should be focused on those whose chance of passing was highest. Some 50,000 students nationally, mainly from working-class homes, were denied access to this examination. Sir John Cassells, director of the National Commission on Education established in 1991 to review education and training, observed that one third of the nation's youth was being educationally failed, leaving school with poor qualifications or none at all, particularly in inner-city areas: 'What seems to be happening is that schools have been responding to the publication of league tables by wanting as many people to pass as possible. If more teacher time is spent on getting pupils through, the less likely pupils don't get as much'. Don Foster, Liberal Democrat education spokesman commented: 'Too many young people's futures are being sacrificed on the altar of Tory league tables and market forces in education. Fear of these tables is leaving less able pupils in a class of their own – as far away the exam halls as possible.' [49]

There seems to be little prospect of an end to the deformity of league tables. New Labour have continued with the Conservative policy of running league tables for secondary schools. Not only do such tables fit with New Labour's zeal for the market in all areas of society, they also suit the managerialist approach. League tables can be devised for more and more factors, and more and more targets can be devised, with outputs compared and contrasted. But behind the accompanying facade of moralism, working-class and black young people are being increasingly being denied, and de-selected from, the education and qualifications which they sorely need.

THE STRUGGLE FOR THE MORAL WAY

Schools which struggled to find a more just way of providing education in their communities continued to prevent the developing hegemony of the market system of schooling – while the apologists of the cracked moralism continued to put across their ideas with the support of the established press. Melanie Philips in her book *All Shall Have Prizes* condemned the 'egalitarian tyranny', which, she claimed, had built an 'unstructured prison' around the education of millions of young people.[50] It was the true and 'British way of doing things' that must be restored, with an end to such practices as child-centred learning, the cultivation of the imagination and seeing children as 'meaning makers' or young democrats: 'Democracy is for adults,' she declared, 'Choice is adult behaviour'. Her heroes are not only Philip Lawrence, who 'stood up for goodness and truth', but also the Chief Inspector of OFSTED, a 'lone voice in the upper reaches of the collapse of education of educational values' and enemy of libertarian or child-centred teachers (particularly teachers of English), who are 'helping to knock the moral stuffing out of our culture'. Woodhead was also to prove a hero to New Labour (at least until his resignation in 2000): in September 1998 it gave him a new four-year contract and increased his salary by 34 per cent. At the same time classroom teachers received a 2.6% rise over the previous year. As Thomas Paine wrote two hundred years ago in *The Rights of Man*: 'When extraordinary power and extraordinary pay are allotted to any individual in a government, he becomes the centre, round which every kind of corruption generates and forms.'

Meanwhile in many struggling locations of inner-city Britain, students and their teachers and communities demonstrate the true meanings of morality in their campaigning and efforts to make their school answer to their needs. In east

London over 200 students protested and marched from Forest Gate school to a local park to prevent their schoolmate Natasha Mambelle being deported to Angola, where her mother and brother had been killed.[51] In Sheffield students from Earl Marshal School demonstrated and boycotted classes in protest at the ousting of their headteacher and the stripping away of their governors' powers by the local authority.[52] They raised money through a lunchtime fashion show for a reserve fund to pay for school meals for refugee schoolmates in the light of the impending passage of the Asylum Bill.[53] In May 1996 they boycotted classes again, to secure the removal of an allegedly racist teacher who they claimed had assaulted a Yemeni girl.[54]

In Abraham Moss School in Manchester, students, many from Somali and Bosnian refugee families, raised over £200 for a local man after they had heard that burglars had raided his home. They also gave daily help to their 25 physically disabled colleagues to enable them to make the most of their schooling, and they gave up their lunch hours to support new Vietnamese classmates learning English.[55] In Bradford, determined teachers and parents won the struggle to stop the closure of their local school, Fairfax,[56] and the local community in Haringey, north London, successfully campaigned to save their school being taken over by a government 'educational association'.[57] Nationwide NUT pressure from active members secured additional 'Section 11' funding for young black and arrivant children learning English,[58] and after persistent community resistance in Southall, west London, the Blair Peach school, renamed by the Conservative council when it came to power, regained its former name.[59] Finally in October 1996, 15,000 teachers, governors, parents and school students marched through to streets of London to demand an end to education cuts.[60]

Such events and the motivation behind their organising reveal the true face of morality in education. They involve the values of generosity, community, solidarity, loyalty and co-operation, the determination to gain a just and fulfilling education for all and the will to resist the meanness and selfishness of the market system. They are at the foundation of a true and real understanding of what is right and what is wrong. They uphold the notion of the *inclusive* school rather than the expedient school which subjects itself to market forces and which is too frightened or too rigid to be challenged. The moral school is the school which looks upon challenge as an opportunity to grow, to become more human and embracing. It rejects the immoral moralism of the market. It has its own models of excellence and dedication, among teachers such as Blair Peach, and it reaches out to the world through its curriculum in a celebration of its internationalism, multilingualism and a search for the knowledge, skills, imagination and reflection that will create real possibilities for the betterment of all students. Its cause is its community and the development of *all* the people that community holds, not its place in the league tables or a dream of the formulaic perfection of its OFSTED inspection. These are the values that matter and endure – worlds away from the Chief Inspector's orders or Dr Tate's prescriptions. They are the values that will cherish the present and construct the future without authoritarianism and hypocrisy, because they are values in process, towards what Frantz Fanon called an 'actional' education, where those who educate do so 'preserving in all their relations a respect for the basic human values that constitute a human world, the prime task of those who having taken thought, prepare to act'.[60] In this way, the word and the world are unified, knowledge bonds with practice and is made, tested through human action and service, and affirmed anywhere where ordinary people meet, learn from each other, act and struggle. They are the values of the inclusive school, to which we now turn.

REFERENCES

1. *The Daily Express*, 16.1.96.
2. *The Guardian*, 16.1.96.
3. *Daily Express*, 16.1.96.
4. *Guardian*, 16.1.96.
5. *Times Educational Supplement*, 21.7.95.
6. *Daily Express*, 15.1.96.
7. *The Times*, 31.10.96.
8. *Guardian*, 20.11.96.
9. *The Times*, 31.10.96.
10. *Independent on Sunday*, 24.11.96.
11. *Morning Star*, 16.1.96.
12. *Guardian*, 24.10.95.
13. *Times*, 31.10.96.
14. *European Race Audit*, August 1996.
15. *CARF*, October/November 1996.
16. *European Race Audit*, August 1996.
17. *CARF*, December 1996/January 1997.
18. *European Race Audit*, December 1996.
19. *The Times*, 31.10.96.
20. *Yorkshire Post*, 22.10.96.
21. *Guardian*, 22.10.96.
22. *The Times*, 9.12.96.
23. *Daily Telegraph*, 10.12.95.
24. *Yorkshire Post*, 22.10.96.
25. *Daily Mirror*, 21.10.96.
26. Bob Franklin and Julian Petley, 'Killing the Age of Innocence: Newspaper reporting of the death of Jamie Bulger' in Jane Pilcher and Stephen Wagg, *Thatcher's Children*, Falmer Press, London 1996.

27. *Sunday Mirror*, 8.12.96.
28. *Times Educational Supplement*, 15.11.95.
29. *Daily Mail*, 22.10.96.
30. *Daily Express*, 22.10.96.
31. *The Times*, 24.4.96.
32. *Times Educational Supplement*, 15.11.96.
33. *Times Educational Supplement*, 1.11.96.
34. *Times Educational Supplement*, 15.11.96.
35. *Guardian*, 11.9.96.
36. *Guardian*, 13.11.96.
37. *Guardian Education*, 3.12.96.
38. *Morning Star*, 14.9.96.
39. *Newsnight BBC2*, 24 October and *BBC Breakfast TV*, 20 October 1996.
40. *Independent on Sunday*, 28.10.96.
41. *Times Educational Supplement*, 1.11.96.
42. *Guardian*, 11.9.96.
43. *Morning Star*, 3.9.96.
44. *Times Educational Supplement*, 1.11.96.
45. *Morning Star*, 11.12.96.
46. *Times Educational Supplement*, 1.11.96.
47. *Guardian*, 4 .9.96.
48. *Sun*, 30.10.96.
49. *Independent*, 21.8.96.
50. Melanie Philips, *All Shall Have Prizes*, London 1996.
51. *CARF*, June/July 1996.
52. *Star*, Sheffield, 9.2.96 and Yorkshire Post, 9.2.96. Also 'OFSTEDed, Blunketted and Permanently Excluded' by Chris Searle, *Race and Class* Vol.38, No.1, July 1996.
53. *Star*, Sheffield, 1012.96.
54. *Star*, Sheffield, 21.5.96.
55. *Times Educational Supplement*, 1.11.96.
56. *Teacher*, October/November 1996.

57. *Teacher*, July/August 1996.
58. *Teacher*, July/August 1996.
59. *Teacher*, January/February 1995.
60. *Teacher*, November 1996.
61. Frantz Fanon, *Black Skin, White Masks*, London 1986.

CHAPTER 6

'The Whole Page'
Features of the Inclusive School

For many years teachers assumed that the idea of 'inclusivity' was an integral dimension of the 'comprehensive' school. How could a comprehensive school not be inclusive? Surely that was its very reason for being: that it was the educational hub of any community, the learning rendezvous for all its children, freely open to its community for wider use, a vital centre of local life and development. This projection of the comprehensive school came to me most forcibly in the campaign waged by teachers, students and community in 1990-91 to stop the closure of Earl Marshal School after the local education authority had produced a 'schools plan' for north-east Sheffield which proposed the school's closure as a likely option. At a crowded campaign meeting, a senior Pakistani governor described the school as the community's 'second home'. Those who were present at the meeting gasped and clapped. For there can surely be no more fitting metaphor for a community-based comprehensive and inclusive school. It has that degree of local significance for all who use it or teach and learn in it. It is a home of learning, an emotional centre of local democratic life wrapped up in the identity of its community. It is there for all, to offer stability and also hope, care and the promise of betterment.

Strong words, yet ones that are necessary in a book about exclusion. In the present context schools are frequently being judged as failures, with a barrage of public shaming, to be subsequently torn apart, closed down, and then discarded, with 'new' schools with new names then established on the same premises a few weeks later. Instead of seeking to support the needs of inner-city schools, the Government punishes them for failing to conform to its targets. This was the fate of Earl Marshal school, which was closed in July 1998. A new school, 'Fir Vale', opened in September 1998 on the same site, the flagship school of a partly business-financed Education Action Zone. Such schools have no stability, are allowed no roots, no thoughts of permanence, if they stand inside an inner city. Their very existence is subject to OFSTED formulas, inspectorial interventions, capricious business interests, and the opportunism of shrinking LEAs and expanding government quangos. They struggle under 'special measures' – another punishment for failure – their anxious school leaderships imposing on teachers a huge burden of paperwork, lesson plans and re-bureaucratisation in the form of the required 'action plans' for rapid improvement. Fine teachers are bent over with the weight of such an incubus, their students forced into the behaviourist madness of regimented 'school improvement' strategies, school uniform regulations, more and more testing and modes of selection and control.

As the new managerialism among headteachers is promoted by government as a vehicle for 'raising educational standards', *The Times* of 4 November 1998 reported that a cross-party Education and Employment Select Committee of MPs was advocating that heads and deputy heads 'could be replaced by high-flyers from the financial sector'. An approving editorial in the same issue acknowledged that 'the language and practices of the boardroom are steadily seeping into the classroom' – and recommended that 'like successful chief executives, headteachers should be rewarded if their school results improve year on year'. Such are the undemocratic instruments of the 'standards' revolution, used primarily to ensure more A-stars and increases in the A-C grades of GCSE to hoist progress up the league tables, while those unlikely to succeed are offered less and less and excluded more and more from the mainstream learning benefits of school life – with the 1998 student failure rate rising by 50 per cent and 120,000 student entrants labelled as 'unclassified'.[1]

These 120,000 'unclassified' or the 250,000 at 'status zero' (see p64) – effectively a new generation of 'secondary-moderners' – what has a decade of state education meant to them, or done for them? It has discarded and rejected them through an irresponsible market system of education, guided in its curriculum policy by a culture of narrowing cultural nationalism. This all adds up to a national educational structure in which exclusion is not a mere marginal irritation, but is a central and integral part of the system. The 10,404 young people who appear on the official records as 'permanently excluded' from schools – and all those who are not officially reported – are a disturbing human symptom of this reality. Furthermore, in a 1993 *Panorama* programme, a BBC-commissioned MORI survey estimated that the number of school students out of school on both 'official' and unofficial exclusion was close to six times the number being formally recorded at that time – 66,000. And this state of affairs is almost certainly very similar at the time of writing.

Those who are categorised out of the system at 'status zero' or 'unclassified' are, every one of them, human beings of precious potential and brainpower. They are the foundation of exclusion on which the British education system, with its market orientation and built-in wastage, has been re-erected since 1988. As more achieve their A-stars at the top, more gain nothing at the bottom, and most of these are children of the working class, white and black, as are those who are formally excluded. Yet many of these young people are not simply 'victims' of the system. They have made deliberate choices along the way of school, choices of rejection and intolerance of exclusion. Sometimes their disaffection has caused them genuine frustration, anger and suffering. They have felt a real pain as their own lives, histories, heroes, languages, cultures and faiths have been dismissed or marginalised. Sometimes they have felt the 'draught' of teacher racism – and when asked to explain it have found it difficult to articulate a 'feeling'. They have rebelled against school authoritarianism. When their anger has broken out it has put them into trouble, serious trouble. Their resistance has been desperate, emotive, sometimes anarchic, and it has frequently been confronted with a system that is implacable, bureaucratic and incapable of showing the slightest flicker of rational understanding. Its sophisticated apparatus of pastoral provision and 'special needs' resources have often become the mechanisms that have defined the category of rejection of the 'excluded' student: 'educationally sub-normal', 'maladjusted', 'emotionally disturbed'. A whole history of social rejection and marginalisation lies embedded within these terms.

THEMES OF INCLUSION

I want to pare the characteristics of an 'inclusive school' down to five major dimensions, all essential strands of educational democracy, from which I believe all other necessary details emerge. As I am writing in the particular context of a market education system, the main thematic principle has to be defiance of the market. An 'inclusive school' cannot exist if it accommodates itself within a system of market competition and rivalry. Such a system needs its failures to balance its successes, its unsaleable goods to complement its retail profits. I remember as a child walking around the almost deserted streets of Romford market place after Saturday's market. The waste was everywhere, left in putrid piles in the gutters, in damp, collapsing cardboard boxes as the hoses washed down the pavements, all to be shovelled and forked on to refuse wagons in the hour of dusk. A telling image for me then, and now not without its symbolism.

Secondly, and fundamentally, there is the question of curriculum. An inclusive curriculum starts from the breadth of the lives of its students and their communities, and goes on broadening. The inclusive school is a school of the world: it does not stop at being a school of the nation. Its curriculum includes the narratives of all who impact upon it. It does not restrict itself to a canon of established work – it is a tool of discovery, a creative mechanism by which the autobiographies of all the lives of the school can be told and explored; all their histories, languages, beliefs and skills. It goes beyond the personal, institutional and national boundaries that it breaks through.

Thirdly, the inclusive school is a critical school. It takes nothing from above on trust. It uses the apparatus of knowledge and curriculum to scrutinise; and uses its languages to examine and critique. It educates young scholars – who are also young critics – and teaches them, to quote Brecht, to 'grab hold of a book. It's a weapon. You must take over the leadership.' [2]

Fourthly, there is the relationship the 'inclusive school' has with its community of learners and their families, who often become the teachers of the teachers. This community offers a depth of support, involvement, knowledge and governance which can build such a symbiosis that school and community become one.

Fifthly, there is the dimension of a school's ethos: an inclusive school should be a place of trust, of care and intercommunal friendship. It should be a bulwark against division and communalism, a centre of active participation and democracy, where its constituents have their own fora – and, most pertinent, it should be a centre of growth in co-operative empowerment among students and teachers, and an incentive towards the empowerment of the community it serves.

DEFIANCE OF THE MARKET

When I became headteacher of Earl Marshal School in 1990, I worked with the governors to try to make the school as inclusive as possible. As a symbol of this aim we established a new letterhead and watchwords for the school. Beside three doves, black and white, soaring from an open book, the school's name was printed *Earl Marshal Comprehensive School*, and the phrase 'For excellence and community'. Out of over thirty secondary and nominally comprehensive schools in Sheffield at the time, ours was the only one to openly and unequivocally call ourselves a 'comprehensive school' and emblazon it on everything issued by the school. We were proud to be comprehensive, and determined to 'make a statement' through it – at a time when many schools were retreating from comprehensive principles in the face of intense market pressures.

One tempting response to the market is image-making, promoting a school as if it were a product, emphasising 'how things look' rather than how things really are. As schools compete for potential students, many have resorted to sheer salesmanship to appear more attractive to parents. This can take the form of the introduction of 'dress codes' and uniforms or sacrificing resources for struggling students in favour of those more likely to achieve impressive examination results. Thus the school's 'successful' image is boosted. It can mean certain subjects being dropped or sidelined from the mainstream curriculum (sometimes first languages like Panjabi, Bengali or Arabic have been abandoned in this way), with their teachers facing dismissal or redundancy when their particular sources of funding are lost to the school budget. These languages need to be taught, sustained and developed in the inclusive school, regardless of the intimidation of the market. In the same way the school may need to use its own budget to help finance its community's supplementary classes. In the case of Earl Marshal, the school always paid the caretaker's overtime, the lighting and heating bills and extra cleaning costs for all community education activities in the school.

Market success is judged by examination success, which means success in the numbers of students that achieve C grade or above in GCSE (the equivalent of a former O-level pass). This has meant that many market-driven schools have felt the pressure (often generated by officers and inspectors of their local education authority) to concentrate resources on students likely to achieve at least a 'C' pass, or who are on the 'borderline' between grades D and C, leaving those likely to gain passes below that level to receive less attention. No genuine comprehensive school that follows inclusive policies and practices could ever operate such anti-student strategies. Examination success must certainly be seen as an important aspect of school success, but it should never be judged as the whole story of school excellence. Internal school budgeting is a nightmare for an inner-city school, but the solution does not lie in becoming market-driven, even though there are strong pressures pushing schools in this direction, since funding is less and less allocated on a needs basis: large amounts of external funding for schools have been removed, both from the Home Office (Section 11 funding for teaching posts expressly established to serve black communities) and from LEAs (in particular the reduction of funding for the 250,000 children in English schools who are statemented as having 'special educational needs').[3] This means that budgets have been impossibly stretched.

A school signals its commitment to inclusive education and the proper educational care of its constituent communities if it ensures that its priority funding covers those vital areas of school life and student need. It reinforces this commitment by ensuring that there is an effective organisation and the professional expertise within the school to prevent crisis situations which, in other institutions, might lead for calls for students to be excluded. This could mean investing in the post of school counsellor, for example, or bilingual community liaison teachers. It could mean that a particular bilingual subject teacher might be allocated two days a week to make home visits or to work with community organisations alongside students 'on the edge' of school life. None of these posts appeal to market priorities yet they may be essential to save the educational lives of any number of disaffected students.

When Earl Marshal was losing worrying numbers of truanting students to the temptations of gambling machines in a local Yemeni café, we realised we had to enlist the help of the café's proprietor and regular customers – who were mainly unemployed Yemeni ex-steelworkers, who had been made redundant during the collapse of Sheffield's steel industry around the early 1980s. They were mostly middle-aged or older, and illiterate in English, making it extremely difficult for them to find re-employment. We saw a dual need. Our students who truanted to use the café needed to be intercepted and persuaded to return to school. And if we could offer some of its regular customers and our neighbours some literacy classes, we would also be making a positive contribution to their future. So a creative and enthusiastic Pakistani teacher of Urdu who split his timetable as a Community Liaison Teacher, suggested that he spend several hours a week in the café teaching its customers basic English. The owner was enthusiastic, the classes were well attended, and the student users and would-be gamblers kept well away, some of them even returning to school and pursuing their studies with greater commitment. Here was an example of budget use being initiated by school and community need, and certainly not by market considerations. By such strategies too, we found support in the place we really needed and wanted it – in the streets and estates around the school. The café's customers became the school's allies, encouraging truants to return to their classes. In the end, the community became our true OFSTED; our budget was there to serve them, not the spin and image of market favour.

Succumbing to the market creates the worst of directions for inner-city schools. Managements begin to channel all their activities towards the next OFSTED inspection. Managerialism becomes rampant: good headteachers become sucked into behaviourist false remedies, from 'total quality management' strategies to quasi-Skinnerian school improvement techniques. Useful and reflective in-service sessions which should be extending the imaginative pedagogy and self-critical practice of teachers are overwhelmed and replaced by tedious functional sessions on 'How to prepare for an OFSTED inspection', if one is imminent, or 'How to implement an OFSTED Action Plan' if one has just been done. Teacher thinking and development is reduced to mere functionalism. The professional genius that teachers regularly generate in conceptualising original ideas and creative classroom processes is reduced to aping the formulaic approaches in the OFSTED handbook and the required follow-up to inspections. The inclusive school rejects this anti-developmental process. It ensures that its in-service work correlates with its own perceived professional needs for its students and communities. There is little enough money in any school budget for valuable in-service work. It needs to be directed towards teacher activities that creatively and usefully motivate those who take part.

The 1988 Education Reform Act devolved school budgets, creating local management of schools with the declared purpose of enabling more school-based decision-making, while at the same time removing the rights of schools to set their own curriculum priorities, yoking them to OFSTED and a centralised curriculum. If a comprehensive school gains the trust of its local communities, even in the darkest phases of open enrolment when many of the residents of its former catchment area are looking further afield for their children's schooling, it can still survive and prosper with committed teachers and governors and a loyal parent constituency. The market system has created a haemorrhaging of local comprehensive schools in working-class neighbourhoods, but that may not be inevitable. Defiance of the market, sometimes involving the taking of tactical risks to address the declared needs of the communities, including a refusal to permanently exclude their children, can inspire popular support rather than diminish it; and this can make it more difficult for a government quango like OFSTED, or a frightened LEA, to close a school down or intimidate it out of its inclusive commitments.

In their survey of the first three decades of comprehensive education, *Thirty Years On: Is Comprehensive Education Alive and Well or Struggling to Survive?*, Caroline Benn and Clyde Chitty demonstrate how two essential features of comprehensive education are slipping off the agenda under these pressures. 'The use of mixed ability groupings', they observe, 'has become a relatively neglected and uninspiring issue in recent years'.[4] They note how few schools employ such groupings beyond Year 7. They also report that 'work in schools and colleges on equal opportunities had lapsed generally'. The inclusive school cannot be a streaming school; neither can it allow the practice of antiracist, anti-sexist teaching to be anything less than a constant priority. The 'market' in education has made these essential features of school life nothing more than a trimming in many schools, and non-existent in many more. Some schools simply 'borrow a policy' on Equal Opportunities from another one, to impress OFSTED when their inspection comes around. The inclusive school embraces these curriculum dimensions as imperatives, and builds its whole-school practices and ethos upon them, making mixed ability, antiracist, anti-sexist and anti-homophobic teaching essential bricks and mortar.

THE INCLUSIVE CURRICULUM
The inclusive curriculum begins in the real lives of students. It starts in their own word universes, and travels out from there, encompassing the world. And that world, in all its cosmopolitanism may already be sitting at the desks in their classrooms. It is a tragic contradiction in the British education system that, at a time when the population of schools has never been broader, more internationalist, more full of learning opportunities offered by languages, histories, beliefs and cultures not available before in British classrooms – and full

of so much vibrancy, wisdom and cognitive opportunity – the curriculum prescribed in schools is so narrow and restrictive. And so governed by nationalism and xenophobia and the wish to impose, in Dr Tate's words, the Englishness of 'a strong majority culture', when the world is at work in every inner-city classroom.

The inclusive curriculum, taking from so much that is world-wide and internationalist, cannot accommodate itself to the confines of the National Curriculum. Young people whose lives span the world will never be content with only the nation as the context and definition of their knowledge, particularly when that national perspective excludes their own language, history and culture. The realisation of this curriculum exclusion in the consciousness of many thousands of inner city young people creates hurt and indignation, which is often difficult to deal with. It can be easier to wear a mask than to show rebellion and anger. Their country, their school, and many of their teachers are rendering them invisible, or presenting a caricature of their identities and experience and those of their communities. How many of their teachers critically discussed with their students in assemblies and classrooms the grotesque representations of Irish people in the 'Irish' episodes of the mass audience *East Enders* in September 1997? What did Irish families and their children at schools in England feel? How did schools throughout England respond to the warped interpretations of history given in a mass-release film like *Amistad* (1998), where the British are portrayed as the 'good guys' of history who killed off the slave trade? What do the black young people of Caribbean and African origins, with the historical memory of slavery – and resistance to slavery – still carried in their English surnames, make of such a narrative? Is the school's history curriculum there to help them understand the truths and falsities of history?

Above all, the inclusive curriculum is a critical curriculum, putting everything under scrutiny, generating a critical, questioning attitude to anything which passes as 'knowledge'. In this sense it is anti-prescriptive. It cannot be 'delivered' because it stands at the side of 'prescribed' knowledge in order to critically read and interpret it. The notion of teachers being the 'deliverers' of curriculum conforms to a view of filling the empty mind-vessels of youth, the 'banking' concept of education which literacy educators like Paulo Freire analysed and discredited thirty years ago.

The inclusive curriculum is both generative and situational. It begins by being made by students and teachers – from the real lives, streets, histories, families, languages, cultures and preoccupations of the students, and the creative curriculum development and classroom scholarship of the teachers with whom they share knowledge, insight and realisation. In contrast, the 'delivered' curriculum, mechanistically imposed, quickly becomes moribund. The inclusive curriculum begins as autobiography and moves outwards, always retaining relevance and sparking motivation and meaning. To travel there means beginning in the child's world and voyaging out. For to begin with critical insight of the student's world and word universe is not to ghettoise the curriculum. Rather it gives a foundation of discovery, knowledge and self-confidence in the students' own lives, which enables them to connect with and share understandings of the world outside. These can be recognised and rewarded through success in national examinations, leading to accreditation, qualifications and higher education that are central to the adult world and the student's place in it. Thus the inclusive school aims also to be the high-achieving school. There is no contradiction between its inclusivity, its humanity and its excellence as a centre of teaching and learning.

To explore history, its conflicts, divisions and wars, why start from a textbook when you can start from the lives of children? The question can be answered by reading examples of work generated by students starting from their own lives. The value of such an approach is as evident in the quality of the work as in the worlds it reveals. Take this poem, for example, about the conflict in Yemen, by a girl who has lived there and seen its strife and pain and is imploring reflection and answers. Why not begin with these words, from her Arabian universe, now a part of a south Yorkshire classroom?

Searching for Aden
Since I was born
I saw a great world, full of love and beauty.
Since I was born
I used to breathe fresh and clean air,
I used to be hugged by soft arms
Those arms that belong to my mother, Aden.

Aden was a beautiful mother,
Full of love, beauty, peace and freedom.

Aden who built all her people
Aden who loved all her people
Aden who cared for all her people.

Since I was born
Aden taught me how to love her
How to protect her
How to look after her
And I never thought of that day,
That terrible day
On that day when all my dreams were shattered.

I thought life was easy and free,
But suddenly
I heard a big, strong and terrible explosion,
A strong explosion which shocked Aden.

Since that day, hell started
Something unbelievable happened.
Everyone was killing the other
Everyone was attacking the other
Brothers were fighting against each other,
But why?
Aden never told us to kill our brothers,
Aden told us to love our brothers.
Suddenly
The blue sea changed into red sea
Full of blood –
Can anyone imagine a red sea?

We used to call Yemen 'the Happy Yemen'.
That is in the past.
Now everything has changed.
Aden was lost – killed by her people
Who taught them how to love and live
Why are we fighting?
Why are we killing?
Why are we hating?
We are starting to forget that we are Muslims
We are starting to forget that we are human beings,
Human beings who were created to love and live
To live in peace and freedom.
Can anyone answer these questions?
Not only Yemen has killing and fighting
But it's throughout the world.

Can anyone stop the killing and fighting?
Can we live in peace?
Can we bring Aden back?
I must fight to bring Aden back
Because no one can live without her mother.
Aden will be back as before
And better than before.

Safa[5]

'Searching for Aden', with its central metaphor of the mother, its narrative of tragedy, war and communalism, its deep-seeking questions, is a sharp and telling text for any inner-city school. It speaks to the agony of many sectarian conflicts, in history and in contemporary life, in Asia, Africa and Europe, in conflicts large and small – even those liable to break out in any urban playground. It comes straight from the lives of its students and convincingly illustrates a central theme from Apple and Beane's *Democratic Schools: Lessons from the Chalk Face*, that 'knowledge is that which is intimately connected to the communities and biographies of real people'.[6] The intimate, personal and autobiographical knowledge conveyed in this poem does not diminish the 'dominant' knowledge conveyed in that national curriculum. It gives it a new perspective, a new immediacy – it supplements and enhances other readings of history, opens up key questions about it and subjects it to new experience – the real and visceral experience of the person sitting at the next desk to you. It shows that prescribed, handed-down knowledge has to be validated by real lives. It is through such scrutiny and validation that both teachers and students can examine its truth. This is the knowledge offered by the inclusive school, and the means by which those working in the school investigate complex experiences: through the imaginative basis of empathy, and the rational process of scepticism. This same 'empathy and scepticism' grounded in 'a curriculum of questions' that become the foundation of the students' portfolio work at Central Park East Secondary School in New York – also described in Apple and Beane's book.

Safa's poem invites a reading which is socio-historical: why did these events happen in Aden? What caused them? What relationship do they bear to situations in the Balkans, in Northern Ireland, in Somalia or Rwanda? Or a reading which is geographical and political: where is Aden? Why is it politically, economically and positionally so crucial to Europe and the West? Why is it divided? What is its connection to Britain and its former empire? Or a reading which is sociological: why are the people of Aden in Britain, in Sheffield? What has been the Yemeni migrant experience? How have Yemenis in Britain held on to their language, their religion and culture, their community life? How have they lived with other communities in a large industrial city? What about other communities too – Pakistanis, Somalis, Caribbeans? How have the different generations adapted and changed? Or an aesthetic reading: how does Safa's *Searching for Aden* work as a poem? What imagery does it employ? Why are there so many rhetorical and unanswered questions? What is this 'search' to which the title refers? Are there other poems we can find with similar themes written by other poets from other countries in other languages? Can we find related paradigms within the work of other Arabic poets like Darwish or Adonis? Are there poems with such narratives of searching by contemporary English poets?

Through the curriculum-making skills of the creative teacher, knowledge in the inclusive school is built, word-by-word, story-by-story, real life by real life, question, reflection and the beginning of answers, shared in the classroom – the generating-place of knowledge. These are answers not from the textbook, or 'delivered' through prescriptive classroom formulae, but *created* through told and authentic experience which families and communities know is true because they have lived it.

I have selected *Searching for Aden* from hundreds of creative narratives in prose and poetry invented by students of Earl Marshal School, many of them published in a series of anthologies produced by the school. Each one is a curriculum starting point. Another example is fourteen-year-old Afroz's story of her family's Hadj to Mecca and the muslim holy places. She writes with a sense of human marvel, humour and realism that is similar to Chaucer's in his fifteenth century *Canterbury Tales*, an earlier collective human story of pilgrimage – underlining the truth, too, that more people worship in mosques in England today than in churches. For Afroz the Hadj is a stimulus for learning and discovery, an essential part of the living curriculum of the inclusive school.

> *Mecca, Medina and our Haj*
> In the morning my uncle, mum, me and my grandma woke up at 4.00 am. We prayed and had something to eat, then it was time to go. We shot off at 6.00 am, the minibus was waiting outside. My auntie and grandma started to cry. Me and my uncle laughed at them and said, 'we're not going to World War 3, we're going to a fabulous place!'
>
> Then we were getting ready to go on the plane we picked up our luggage and went to get our passports stamped. We got on the aeroplane. My grandma argued and said, 'I'm not sitting alone,' because there were only three seats in a row and we were four people. When we got there, from the sky I could see the wonderful lights of Mecca. It looked so beautiful from

the top, maybe because it was dark. We were told to fasten our seat belts.

Then the aeroplane came down. As soon as we got off the plane some buses came, we had to go in these. From the bus I could see some aeroplanes coming down, and some going up but I'd noticed that only our plane was standing still. That means we were the first ones to get off. It looked so funny! Actually everyone did. Because I couldn't see such a thing as head hair I burst out laughing. 'Why are you laughing?' my mum asked. I said oh, 'I just felt so sleepy.' I wasn't too happy to come in the first place because I'd miss my school, but then it got different. I really started to enjoy it.

When we got to the Mosque I couldn't stop looking at it. I mean it was so beautifully clean and neat. It was shining from all over, and half of it was made of real gold.

When we prayed, all the world in Saudi Arabia are at the Mosque. We pray together, and if a person gets late they'll start praying on the road because all the traffic is stopped. It is so quiet, so scary when we pray, because there's no such thing as sound when we're praying. When we got out of the Mosque we bought some food, we tidied our luggage and we all had a bath except me, because people were taking very long in the bathroom.

There were only two bathrooms, one was for men and one was for women. Everybody stank because they were sweating. Everyone in the house went to sleep. We went and had a shower. It was very quiet and it was very, very hot too, and the water was warm. It smelled in the bathroom and the toilet was awful. It didn't smell or anything but it was the toilet – you had to sit on the floor. The good news was that there was a shower, but sometimes with warm water or boiling hot. We had to go to Medina in about twelve days. Finally the days went past and it was time to go. We got our luggage and put it on the coach. The journey was for twelve hours. We set off at 10.00 am and stopped on the way to pray in Mosques. There were still eight hours to go.

We prayed, and before you pray you clean yourself, you wash your arms, face and feet. Suddenly in the place where the women were cleaning themselves, the lights went off and when the lights came back on after about five minutes, I looked in the sink. There were grasshoppers and lizards, I screamed. It was a very big sink. The taps just went on and on to God knows where, at least a hundred people can wash themselves, then we went to the place where our prophet's daughter's Mosque was. We prayed inside there, then went back on the bus. It was dark, the time was about 5.00 p.m. Then we went back on the coach. When we got to Medina it was morning, and it was even hotter than it is in Mecca.

We went to where the devils frightened our prophet and his relatives. We prayed there. We also saw the place where our prophet's daughters', nephews', sons were buried and also found out that whoever dies in Saudi Arabia gets buried there, and I thought what a fortunate person who dies there! I also saw my prophet's garden which was full of fresh dates and also smelt gorgeous and was very, very neat. No one was allowed in these kinds of places because they said we're not good enough or capable to touch these things. I saw the two mountains that have walked from heaven to the world, and that's where our prophet used to hide when the devils wanted to kill him. If our prophet worked it, he could have had anything done.

We prayed in the mountains, then we went back to Mecca, and on the way there everyone needed to cover their hair and get all dressed up correctly. We came to Mecca and didn't rest a bit. We went straight to the Mosque and drank the very special water. They say the holy water came by a miracle, the devils wouldn't give our prophet' s daughter's sons water. The sons cried and rubbed their feet on the ground. The holy water came out and the devil got surprised. Until now the water comes out of that well. In the mosque are coolers with very clean fresh water that is called 'Zam Zam.' The Mosque is so cool and cold and you could just keep on drinking that water, even if you drink about six or seven glasses or beakers. You'll still think you've drunk nothing.

After we came back from the Mosque, we had a bath, we got ready for the very five hard days in the tents. Believe me, it is so, so hot. It seems the sun's on the floor. Then afterwards the five days went past we went to a place where all the world's going to be one day. You have to pray exactly five times. It is also very hot there.

We came back to Mecca and went to the Mosque to say hello to the black stone. We were very very thirsty. We made the last visit to the Mosque and we all started to cry, 'our prophet's in heaven, and the devil's in hell!' It was all like a dream. It was absolutely amazing. I'd love to go again and I hope every human being goes there.

Afroz[7]

Why are such rich educational and life-enhancing experiences still so frequently regarded by schools as 'interruptions' to education, dismissed as a nuisance rather than nourished for their learning value? If the student had made a long journey to France or Germany, perhaps the school's view would be more positive. For the echoes here are non-Christian and non-European as well as English. The truth is that the inclusive school embraces all these experiences. In the words of black and British St Kitt's-born novelist Caryl Phillips, Britain is now 'the crucible of fusion – of hybridity'; and the inclusive school is the flame for that process. In his preface to his anthology of 'a literature of belonging', *Extravagant Strangers*, Phillips writes:

> The once great colonial power that is Britain has always sought to define her people, and by extension the nation itself, by identifying those who don't belong. As a result, Britain has developed a vision of herself as a nation that is both culturally and ethnically homogeneous, and this vision has made it difficult for some Britons to feel that they have the right to participate fully in the main narrative of British life.[8]

That notion of homogeneity has no validity, as the inclusive inner-city school proves with the stories that it brings forth. Here are extracts from two such stories, both by fifteen-year-old girls. The first tells of the life of her mother and her childhood in a Pakistani village, confronting the death of her own mother. The second is a local story of south Yorkshire, told by a granddaughter about her grandmother. Two girls learning, reflecting, remembering and writing in the same place at the same time, the words inclusive of huge different spaces in the world, yet being forged in one neighbourhood in north-east Sheffield. First, the long, long journey from Shabana:

> Born on 22 June 1951 in a small place in Pakistan called Dadyal, my mother Risheeda Begum has led a very interesting life, even though at times things were very difficult.
>
> My mother lived in Dadyal with her parents, three brothers and two sisters. She was the third youngest. She says that she can't recall that much about her younger years, except that life was utterly brilliant, and she was happy and carefree. Then all of a sudden all that changed, when she was just ten years old. Her mother and some other ladies of the village

went to some cliffs where some kind of unusual plant grew – they used the plant for all sorts of remedies. Her mother was pulling at a plant, which was refusing to come out. Then she slipped, lost her footing and fell down the cliff. My mother says that she can still remember the day clearly as though it just happened yesterday.

At the time that the tragedy happened, my mother was at home helping her sister-in-law (her first older brother's wife). She was making chapatis for the first time in her life. Then there was an uproar outside their house. At first she couldn't understand why there were people standing outside her door crying, but when she finally got the message – she says that all the world turned upside down. She couldn't handle her mother's death. At first, she says, she refused to believe it – 'in my mind I kept saying over and over again – mum's not dead, she's going to walk in through that door, hug me and say she'll never play a joke on me like that again.'

For three days my mother sat near the door waiting for her mother to come home. From all around the village people came to pay condolences. She recalls how all her brothers and sisters cried, and she didn't shed a tear. On the fourth day after her mother's death, my mother said her sister-in-law grabbed her by the shoulders, shook her hard and screamed the words, 'Your mother is dead, why don't you cry for god's sake?' That's when the tears came and they wouldn't stop.

After the tears stopped, my mother became angry, and the angrier she got the more rebellious she became. She refused point blank to listen to the elders. Her father had become withdrawn himself. He didn't know how to handle his daughter, so he talked to her only when he thought it necessary. Her older sister, who was married, tried to make my mother see reason, but it didn't work. The rebelliousness carried on for quite a few months, until, my mum said – one day she just grew up. The incident which made her grow up concerned her father. He had lost interest in all the things around him since his wife's death, so he decided to come to England to work. He told of his decision to his sons, who strongly disagreed because they thought that in his present condition he wasn't capable of going abroad and looking after himself.

But after her father had gone to England, my mother realised how badly she had handled her mother's death. To make up for it she immediately wrote to her dad, telling him that she had grown up and that she was now very sorry for all the extra grief that she had caused him. At this time she was living with her first older brother and his wife. 'They did everything they could possibly do for me,' she says. As the years slowly passed, my mother learned to be happy again although not fully carefree.[9]

And another journey, shorter, but of equally powerful meaning, by Lorraine:

Three years ago I took a journey that meant a lot to me in many different ways. One morning my mother came to me and said that we would have to go to Chesterfield because my grandma was very sick. That morning at about 10.30 my mother and I went to the bus station for the bus to Chesterfield, hoping to get there before dark.

On the bus I sat and chatted to my mother, asking what was wrong and why the big rush. She told me that my grandma was very sick and wanted to see me and her, just in case anything terrible suddenly happened to her. I knew that my mother meant death and that this chat was upsetting her, so I got comfy on my seat and fell asleep.

My mum woke me up after what seemed like a couple of hours for we were now in Chesterfield. We got into the taxi and sat quietly for the whole journey. We got out of the cab, my mother paid the driver and then he drove away. 'Is this where Grandma lives?' I asked my mum. She turned to me and smiled. 'Yes love, grandma's house is just that one house standing on its own over there.' My mother pointed and I followed her direction to where she was pointing. Grandma's house looked like an antique dolls' house. It had red velvet curtains, fancy arched nets, a plant in every window and a lovely-looking green lawn surrounded by white steel fencing.

My mother and I walked up to the white steel gate and opened it. We followed the long path until we came to a little light-brown varnished door with a shining gold letter box. My Uncle Mark answered the door. He greeted us by giving me a big hug. My mother asked how grandma was. 'Not so good,' replied my uncle. He took my coat and hung it up with four other coats. He led me through to the living room and towards grandma. I ran up to her and hugged her. I couldn't believe that my grandma was going to die. She looked so healthy and well. I sat next to her and talked to her about my school, friends, enemies, teachers, pets I've had and most of all I told her about the journey to get there. Many hours passed before my mother said, 'I'm sorry to disappoint anyone, but Lorraine and I must really be going back now.' It was the most horrible feeling that I ever had, knowing that I might never see my grandma again.

Just before we left she gave me a velvet jewellery box, and inside there were plastic money bags each filled up to the fullest with pounds. My grandma told me that I could do whatever I liked with the money but the jewellery box was to keep for always to remember her by.

I kissed my grandma goodbye and so did my mother. I noticed a tear run down my mother's face but my grandma wiped it away and said, 'Let's leave each other on happy thoughts.' I also felt like crying but I stayed strong and happy, just like grandma wanted me to. We said goodbye to Uncle Mark and left trying to be strong and trying very hard not to cry, but when you leave someone knowing you're never going to see them again, it is very hard.

Days passed by before we heard any news about grandma, (I was hoping for good news). Then on the fourth day we heard that grandma had passed away in her sleep.

We spent the next few days watching TV, crying or sleeping. But we soon got ourselves together and went about our daily routines, which were me going to school and my mother shopping or cooking surprise meals. As for the money from my grandma, I have still got it, safely put away in the bank to this day. I also have the red velvet jewellery box which sits quietly, happily on my windowsill so passers-by can see it.[10]

This unity of creative experience arising from the real lives of students and their families is the hallmark of the inclusive school. Their experience can generate substance in all areas of the curriculum. Issues of neighbourhood health can be studied in Biology – the reduced life expectations of inner-city people, the incidence of heart disease or diabetes, the study of sickle-cell anaemia. Also the industrial illnesses generated by local workplace dangers such as silicosis or deafness caused by working close to industrial hammers in steelworks – and investigations of local housing. There can be projects on local businesses and their development in Business Studies, Sociology lessons with research into local racism and the effects of drug culture on young people or the conducting of surveys into local unemployment. There can be local oral history campaigns in the first languages of schoolside communities. The Law and its attitude to refugees and asylum seekers can be studied; so can alternative technologies in inner-city contexts – an inclusive curriculum begins in the context of the living and working places of the school's constituent communities and works outwards. This is not a soft curricular option. It requires deduction, analysis and rigour in developing skills of investigation and research. It involves collecting evidence, verifying facts and interpreting ideas and assumptions. As the basis of the discipline of learning, it reveals the inclusive school as a scholarly school, where academic apprenticeship is central to classroom work, leading towards accreditation and examination success.

THE CRITICAL SCHOOL (IN AN AGE OF SPIN)

The inclusive school is the critical school, the school that asks questions as much as it seeks answers. This is why it sees its bedrock as the languages that its constituent communities know and use – all of them. For these languages are the tools of its critical foundation: there to analyse and dissect as well as to create lucidity, love and humour. This is particularly so at a time when young people face a dilution and perversion of the meanings of words that is more powerful than anything that has come before. As consumers, they live within a huge market of products, each of which is screaming at them through the mass technologies and ideologies of advertising; but they also live in an age characterised by the phenomenon of political 'spin'.

Enormous amounts of money and resources are directed towards 'spin' – the art of strategic lying. New forms of mystification which dress policy and propaganda as moralism have caused one of Britain's greatest playwrights, Harold Pinter, to write about 'a disease at the very centre of language' whereby 'language is actually employed to keep thought at bay'.[11] The NATO war against Yugoslavia showed this contempt for language in strident ways. The daily press conferences with

NATO publicist Jamie Shea, and his dismissals of the deaths of those being bombed in Belgrade and other Serbian cities as mere 'collateral damage', unfortunate and accidental, tested the limits of chicanery in language. What are our young people to make of his commentary after ten patients died when a sanatorium was struck by NATO bombs in south eastern Serbia: 'There is always a cost to defeat an evil. But the cost of failure to defeat a great evil is far higher'. Mr Shea also reiterated the NATO alliance's insistence on being at the head of any peace-keeping force in Kosovo, saying: 'Our position is clear – no NATO, no go.[12]

'Good', 'evil', the meaning of 'failure' or 'defeat', the making of little soundbite slogans to lodge the language in the minds of the hearers or readers – how much do they need not only the functional dimension of literacy but also the critical dimension? And when General Mike Jackson, the leader of the 'peacekeeping' force in Kosovo, declares that 'the tragedy is that the international community has had to resort to air strikes to reach a settlement', does our respect for language as teachers not force us to pause?[13] What is this 'international community'? Does he not mean NATO, the North Atlantic Treaty Organisation established to prosecute the Cold War with the most powerful weapons the world has ever known? What about all those countries who opposed the war? Are they not also the 'international community'?

The critical school exposes such falsification and misuse of language. During the Gulf War in 1990-91 Earl Marshal School students and their parents were involved in continuous critical debate about the war, with school assemblies and lessons used as forums. Essays and poems were read out in year assemblies about the war, with a common theme of peace. Yemeni parents who had worked in Saudi Arabia and studied the politics of the Arab World invited teachers to a

well-attended after-school in-service session. A group of
Year Eleven girls raised money to help Iraqi student families
at Sheffield University left isolated and destitute by the war.
A local veteran peace campaigner in her seventies who had
spent several weeks in a desert peace camp in the no-man's
land between the armies during the stand-off before the
beginning of the war, came to school and spoke to the
students during assemblies. As Mohammed, aged fifteen,
wrote about the relationship of peace and justice:

> Peace isn't just shaking hands
> It could be facing up to people's demands
> But No!
> They want to rule what is not theirs,
> They make excuses and support millionaires.
> If only they could stop and think on
> their demands
> People could stop killing in the sand
> Peace could remove the gun from the hand.
> Solidarity is the way we should live today,
> And together as one stand up for our say![14]

These are the words of the inclusive school: 'together as
one' is its objective, with the elimination of faction and division in a critical pursuit of the real meanings of its languages
– in events local as well as international. When city journalists exposed the fact that the very wealthy chairman of one of
the two prestigious city football clubs was earning his money
by denying the rights of his employees in the jute mills he
owned near Calcutta, students used their power of poetic
language to reveal his ways. Shahid wrote this in his poem
called 'The Eye of the Needle', seeking to reconcile his
powers of reason and faith:

In Cyril's Indian factories of jute
Workers are dying of starvation.
Still more and more and more
Wages, pensions and benefits unpaid.
Still more and more and more
How can he see people starving day by day?
He must have a heart and feelings
But it looks as if there is a wall
               between us
A wall made of money and greediness
For the rich are always looking for
               more and more
Not the faintest part of their body
               shall be seen in Heaven
The only place where they shall end
is a place of hatred and selfishness.
               And so no blessing.
This wall between rich and poor
               has to be broken.[15]

INCLUSION AND COMMUNITY

An inclusive school is inclusive because, in everything it seeks to achieve, its community is in its heart and brain, the aspirations of its community inspire its every action. Its buildings belong to its community, as do its curriculum, governance and causation. Essential decision-making about a school's budget and curriculum are the responsibility of school governors, who need to be direct representatives of the communities served by the school. They decide who is to come to the school and who is not to come. They are the ultimate arbiters about entry and exclusion policy. It is governors who sit on exclusions appeals and make crucial decisions in the lives of young people and their parents. It is they who decide budget priorities – should precious finances be expended upon building new perimeter fences, employing guards from security firms to keep students and others out, or upon ramps or lifts for disabled students, new bilingual resources, a community liaison or counselling post or sets of Caribbean novels to encourage the excluded to come in? These are questions that only those who use the school should answer. How best can the school offer up its invaluable facilities in the evening or weekends for supplementary classes, language schools, Koranic centres, homework and sports clubs, youth work or computer classes? The waste of closed, bolted and security-guarded school buildings lying unused in the heart of an urban community that yearns for education is one of the most tragic narratives of our cities. Yet my own experience shows that this need not happen. If schools can cover the basic costs of lighting, heating and caretaker overtime and offer a warm and comfortable amenity to its communities, there will be a powerful response. Earl Marshal School hosted an Arabic school for 180 students on Saturdays and Sundays, mainly for Yemeni children, that was staffed, administered and stewarded by the parents and youths of the community on a voluntary basis. It also hosted a nightly Koranic and Urdu class run by Pakistani parents, a class run by Somali mothers and a GCSE enrichment school run by the local Pakistani Muslim Centre. Caribbean cricket enthusiasts organised a cricket centre, with the help of Devon Malcolm, the Jamaican-born and Sheffield-bred international fast bowler. In his autobiography, Malcolm writes about the centre named after him:

> It's situated in an inner-city school called Earl Marshal School and it's there for under-privileged boys and girls of all races – Pakistanis, West Indians, Somalis, Yemenis, Bangladeshis, and

of course, for whites. With such a racial mix at the centre, there's genuine hope that the youngsters will grow up to respect not just their own culture, but others as well. I remember playing for Asian sides in Sheffield, and I enjoyed getting to know about their religion, how they lived their lives. Cricket teaches you respect for others. So the Devon Malcolm Cricket Centre is my attempt to bind young people into one community.[16]

It is the power and support of local communities and the determination and tactical adroitness of community-based school governors that can enable the inclusive school in their neighbourhood to survive, prosper and develop, even in the most unpromising of situations and when the market model of education is at its most rampant. The good work, professionalism, excellence in learning and humanity of the inclusive school will not easily be set aside, even in the intense heat of competition.

The teachers themselves are, of course, vital constituencies of the inclusive school, and such a school needs to ensure that teachers from its participating communities are integral to school life. The school needs their languages, their skills and insights, their life experiences, to reflect those of its students. Thus the recruitment of black colleagues from arrivant communities remains a huge responsibility of the school and, in particular, those entrusted with its governance. All its students must be able to look at their teachers and see mirrors of their own intellectual, creative and leadership potential. And this means that teachers must be drawn from all the school's constituent communities – a priority for the inclusive school. As Nohman, a 13 year old Pakistani student wrote:

> The teacher is the base of everything
> The teacher is the starter of everything

The teacher is the only one who makes
doctors
    engineers
        mechanics
            lawyers.
No matter what a student wants to be
No matter what his ambition is
It can never come true without a teacher!
For the teacher is like sun,
And if there's no sun
There won't be any light –
And if there's no teacher
There won't be any education
Teachers are a sea of education
And without them
You could imagine what life would be like![17]

In the case of Earl Marshal, the community had much to add to the curriculum – with community events eliding into curriculum development for the benefit of all students and those teachers who were open enough to receive knowledge that was fresh from the lives of local communities. Many families were Kashmiri, holding an intense love for their land of origin. When some of these parents suggested a Kashmir exhibition, following successful exhibitions organised by Yemeni and Somali parents, and volunteered to offer the school artefacts, books, posters, clothes, tapes, photographs and newspapers from Kashmir as a catalyst for developing a curriculum theme, the school was happy to respond. Its resources area was soon filled with those exhibits and the exhibition was launched with a party at which there was strong attendance from many communities around the school.

The enthusiasm for knowing about the history, economy and present conflict in Kashmir spread to lessons. Zulfiqar, from a Kashmiri family, expressed his feelings in a strong choric poem:

Beauty and Death in Kashmir
Kashmir, Kashmir!
What should I say about Kashmir?
Shall I talk about the poverty
Or shall I talk about the beauty?
The mountains sparkling
The rivers flowing,
What shall I say?
People dying
Mothers crying
What shall I say?
Pakistan and India fighting
Over this beautiful place,
What shall I say?
Snowtops on the mountains
Forests on the sides of rivers,
What shall I say?
Innocent people are dying,
And those who are dead lie there
In these beautiful mountains
In these riverine places,
What shall I say?
Forts on the ends
of carpets or corn,
What shall I say?
What will become of this place
If the fighting goes on?
What shall I say?

The rivers will flow
The mountains will not die
But the dying will die
The beauty may go
If this fighting does not stop –
Kashmir, Kashmir!
What should I say about
Kashmir?[18]

Zulfiqar's impassioned words had a strong impact upon his fellow students. His white classmate Daniel listened carefully, had closely observed the exhibition, and began to read about this birthplace of so many of his friends:

Kashmir
Beautiful, yet not beautiful.
Lots of flowers, lots of bodies –
Not just from the war
But from hunger, from poverty,
From the curse of fighting.

Some places verdant and fertile,
Wheatfields and miles of golden corn
But some places barren and dry,
Steep mountains, rocky valleys
With long bridges from side to side.

Other parts wet,
Jumpy, swift young rivers,
Slow, tranquil old lakes
Just sitting there peacefully.
Torrential rapids rushing
In a country of houseboats.

But muddy water trickled
Through the streets of poverty
Lives disrupted, lives lost,
Children just sitting and staring
To the end of their broken-down town.
War, guns and death.
Children lost, parents lost.
Crying and shooting –
The saffron flowers are destroyed
And the fields are ruined
By war.[19]

INCLUSION AND EMPOWERMENT

The inclusive school will not be given to us. It will come only from struggle – as comprehensive education was won after many years of campaigning, as corporal punishment was at last abolished, as schools for the 'educationally subnormal' were closed, as 'intelligence tests' and streaming were discredited after years of abuse. As new injustices surface, supported by new forms of racism, but old assertions about eugenics and the ineducability of some sections of the population, this struggle must continue. Even when we think that the old structures have been replaced, Benn and Chitty remind us in their account of comprehensive education that this is far from the truth.[20] Sometimes, forces which have previously been allies for progress in education show their other face and exert backward-looking influence: 'Labour' governments which promote market and divisive education practices, and seek to divide teacher from teacher with 'performance related pay', LEAs which collude with them, or teachers' unions which uphold exclusion and separate schools, units or streams for the demotivated or rebellious. Even as I finish this account, a

NASUWT delegate at their Easter 2001 conference is declaring that 'total inclusion is a form of child abuse', and his leader is claiming that schools must expel 100,000 pupils a year to 'maintain discipline' – a ten-fold increase in permament exclusion.[21] Campaigns against all such forces need to be continuously in motion, and as the Earl Marshal experience shows most emphatically, they will not always be individually successful.

Yet the struggle around progress in education has to be perpetual. The inclusive school must offer its students, teachers and communities a sense of empowerment that derives directly from its ethos – that from unity comes strength and the stamina to continue. In Earl Marshal the 'Founding Principles of the School' document included these essential statements:

Commitment to our Community
Our school belongs to the community, which surrounds it and is served by it. We encourage the highest possible community use of our buildings and resources.

Friendship, Co-operation and Respect
The school can be successful only if its atmosphere and work are guided by friendship and co-operation between students, students and teachers, and between school and community, with the commitment to growth and self-respect and respect for all and between all. This involves:

1. Pride in our internationalism and respect for the life-experiences, languages and cultures of all school members and their families, all citizens of Sheffield, a great city with a powerful past and a dynamic future which all must have a share in shaping.

2. An active opposition to any form of racism or cultural arrogance. We are equals in all aspects of our humanity, and our school must serve as an example of racial justice, inter-community co-operation, understanding and respect.

3. A pride in the achievements and potential of our young women students and a determination that all their ambitions can be realised. Also a respect for all women colleagues and the powerful contribution they make to the life and development of the school.

4. A commitment that the able-bodied and disabled work together in friendship and equality for the benefit and greater education of all.

5. That the friendship of equals can grow between people of different generations: that students and teachers work together as co-operators with mutual respect and self-criticism, without authoritarianism and with an understanding that they can learn from each other and with each other for the benefit and education of all.

Democratic Development

Our school needs to be the centre of community democracy, which encourages discourse, debate, difference and divergence, all within the spirit and development of a critical literacy. To these ends the creative energy of our students arising from the variety of their languages, cultures and life-experiences, need to be valued to the full in structures of democracy, such as school councils. Their involvement in the life and changes of the school needs to be encouraged by their participation in school forums and developmental structures.[22]

This strategy towards empowerment aims to prepare young people to involve themselves in not only self-organised cultural action for justice in the school context, but also to engage them in things that are immediate, local and international, and in issues large and small. To intervene against bullying and name-calling, to support teachers against violent or disruptive behaviour by students in classrooms, corridors or playgrounds – or to criticise teachers if they behave in authoritarian, abusive, sexist or racist ways. It is to prompt them to take action now, to take part in and initiate projects to combat racism or drugs abuse – or to work for a cleaner and healthier neighbourhood environment, to organise and struggle to help prevent the deportation of their schoolmates and to support refugee action. Or wider afield, to respond to internationalist solidarity against tyrannical regimes, abuses of power, or genocide.

It is impossible to conclude writing about the inclusive school, for it has never begun its first day, never called its first assembly or held its first class. It is a process which thousands of teachers, students and parents work within and towards, but it is a process that still has not been accomplished. Yet it stands as the rational future for education, for it is not the margins that we want for our children, but the whole page, on which they can write their lives. The inclusive school can begin to offer them that hope and right. But if the inclusive school is a process, it is a struggle too, and while we dream of it and struggle towards it, politicians, bureaucrats and even some teachers' leaders tear at the structure we work to build. But it exists in our minds, in our imaginations and commitments, and in many of the things we do, large and small, in our schools and classrooms every day. Many teachers conceive it in their days at school, and in their evenings of planning. But it is there most strongly in the consciousness and determination of the young, and it bursts out in new English words, images and energetic rhymes – like those of Nageeb, a Yemeni and now an English boy, in the midst of his thoughts of the future, which he implores us to make real:

If the world was like our school:
Then the sun would shine
And racism would die
Beauty would rise
And the darkness would hide.

Or from Amber's considered couplet:

The school of the world taught me everything I know
The school of the world taught me to love others.

Or from Sajid's energy and huge, young, determination:

Here I come, here I come.
Building my education,
Learning to fight for
Equality.[23]

REFERENCES

1. *The Times*, 27.8.98.
2. From Bertolt Brecht: 'In Praise of Learning', cited in *One for Blair*, Young World Books, London 1989.
3. *Guardian*, 22.10.97.
4. Caroline Benn and Clyde Chitty, *Thirty Years On*, David Fulton, London 1996.
5. Unpublished poem by Safa Mohammed, Earl Marshal School student, 1994.
6. Michael W. Apple and James A. Beane, *Democratic Schools: Lessons from the Chalk Face*, Open University Press, Buckingham 1999.
7. From *School of the World*, Earl Marshal School, Sheffield, 1994.
8. From preface to Caryl Phillips (ed), *Extravagant Strangers*, Faber and Faber, London 1997.